SPECIAL THANKS TO:

PATRICIA EAGLE - my editor - for making sense of my words, correcting my grammar and for being delicate with your criticism. I probably screwed this part up because I added it after you were finished!

LORINN RHODES - our photographer - for snapping so many great pictures of my family.

SUSAN MEESKE - the real talent at the Leadership Difference - for everything.

AND MOST OF ALL...

LORI, BROOKE AND SLADE MITCHELL for supporting the travels and musings of a man pursuing happiness. I love you all so much.

LAUGH AND LEARN!

LIVE AND LEARN
OR DIE STUPID

LIVE AND LEARN OR DIE STUPID!

The Struggle for Happiness

DAVE MITCHELL

Bloomington, IN Milton Keynes, UK

AuthorHouse™
1663 Liberty Drive, Suite 200
Bloomington, IN 47403
www.authorhouse.com
Phone: 1-800-839-8640

AuthorHouse™ UK Ltd.
500 Avebury Boulevard
Central Milton Keynes, MK9 2BE
www.authorhouse.co.uk
Phone: 08001974150

First published by AuthorHouse 7/6/2006

ISBN: 1-4259-4398-5 (sc)
ISBN: 1-4259-4397-7 (dj)

Library of Congress Control Number: 2006905300

Printed in the United States of America
Bloomington, Indiana

This book is printed on acid-free paper.

CONTENTS

PREFACE

(Who the heck is Dave Mitchell?)

I'm just an average guy. Occasionally I feel different, unique, or special in some fundamental way, but when you get right down to it, I recognize we are all pretty similar. Most of us don't walk on hot coals every morning to get motivated about our jobs, although many of us feel about that much pain when we arrive at work. Try as we might, repeating affirmations into the mirror won't change the fact that several of us are quite unsettled by the sight of our own face and body.

No supreme being shows me signs when I am troubled. I am an average person. So are you, I'm guessing. We fall in that broad range called normal. Bottom line, the pursuit of happiness for many of us is the most difficult undertaking we will ever face. In fact, sometimes I think it is impossible for most of us to just be content.

I am not a behavioral psychologist. I am not a self-help guru. I have no magical formula, product, tape series, theory, breakthrough, diet, substance, pill, stretching exercise, or workout regimen. I have not talked to God. Not any of them. I am in no way more qualified to examine the concept of happiness than the clerk at my favorite wine store, or my high school baseball coach, or my father, or the customer service representative at an electronics store, or most of my friends or family. Yet amazingly, it has been these very people that have helped me understand happiness the most.

This book is meant to offer a cathartic experience to us all, most of all me. Life may not be complicated, but it sure can be hard--really hard. The concepts included in these pages work for me because I have had to learn each of them painfully over the course of my 44 years. (Actually, by the time you read this, I may be 60-years-old. Writing books is also hard.) I didn't learn these concepts from a book, yet here I am writing a book now. Why? Because I don't want to forget these lessons; and maybe, just possibly, you have also learned these lessons and wish to not forget them either. We both know how easily, on occasion, we have forgotten lessons, and probably will again.

Therefore, since you and I are going to spend some time together, let me fill you in on who I am. What follows may indeed be far too thorough of a biography. I offer my story, however, as evidence that there is nothing incredibly unusual about me, which I believe proves that I am a credible source of information on the average person's pursuit of happiness. For any of you who feel uninterested in my short biography, I completely understand. If so, skip ahead to Chapter One. I won't take it personally.

LIFE BEYOND GREENUP

Greenup (pronounced like "throw-up," only green. It is comments like this that have rendered me unelectable as a candidate for mayor), where I'm from, is the largest town in the smallest county in Illinois. For as long as I can remember, 1600 people have resided there, at least that's what those green signs on each end of town say. I was born on May 23, 1961, in nearby Mattoon, since Greenup doesn't have a hospital. My youth was pretty typical of small-town America with baseball, bike riding, school, dogs, etc. Mom had a serious problem with drugs and alcohol while I grew up, which most definitely hurt our relationship and explains her curious and obvious absence in the stories that follow. She was a very good person; I just came along at a very bad time. Dad was a committed father, albeit a product of the emotional stoicism that accompanied rural mid-western men who survived the Depression. I can't tell you if my childhood was happy because I don't have a point of comparison. I can tell you, with some confidence, that my childhood preceded my adulthood, except on those often-repeated occasions when they seem to run parallel.

My earliest aspirations were to be a professional baseball player. I would have made it, too, had my career not been cut short at 20-years-old by a severe lack of talent. Like so many others, I was a good player for a small team in the middle of nowhere. I was perfect for the slow pitch softball leagues where the winning team gets the keg of beer (I know. I played softball for beer far too many years).

I did well in high school and my academic aptitude was one of my most marketable qualities early on. My senior year the University of Illinois awarded me a full scholarship that I didn't accept. I was in love. Lisa was the most beautiful girl in our senior class (a total of 76) and she liked *me*! The move to Champaign-Urbana, a 75-mile journey, would surely end our budding romance. I decided instead to commute to Eastern Illinois University for four years and pay for college myself. After graduating from college, however, Lisa left me. Bummer.

My original vocation was in radio and television. I started as a disc jockey while still in my teens and worked at the campus radio station in a variety of management positions. Eventually I got the chance to be a reporter and producer at the local CBS affiliate in Terre Haute, Indiana. It was a fabulous opportunity for a 21-year-old kid. After six months, I quit. Crazy.

After some odd (literally) jobs, I found myself in Chicago almost a year later. My sister, a wonderful human being with a propensity to worry, spearheaded a less-than-subtle campaign to salvage my life. (She's 17 years older than I am and a lifetime without children has left her with a huge and untapped maternal instinct.) With her support, I got a job with Marshall Field's in Chicago and an apartment complete with the type of roaches that only a large city can produce. I refer to this era as my Underwood Chicken Spread years. Other than the occasional frozen pizza, the only thing I ate was this curious, spam-like gelatinous mass--on white bread, of course.

I met Lori in 1984. We worked together. I told her she looked beautiful every day for a year. Literally.

"You look very nice today, Lori," says Dave shyly.

"Thanks," responds Lori, increasingly less amused.

Imagine a repeat of the above two lines every work day for one year.

I never asked her out.

A mutual friend became so frustrated by my snail-like dating strategy that she invited us both out on a double date with her boyfriend--three times. Our friend's efforts finally worked. Lori and I moved in with each other less than three months from our first date and were married one year later, the day after Valentine's Day, 1986.

Lori is the best thing that has ever happened to me. I know that sounds like the inside of a greeting card. Still, I mean it. This fun and charming woman has the most joyous spirit I have ever encountered. I love her more than life itself. I cry while watching bad romantic movies on planes because I think of my love for her. My guess is I fall right behind Lori's horses in her order of affection. That's very high.

In 1990, when Lori was eight months pregnant with our first child and I was a rising star in the Marshall Field's training and development department, we discovered that we were not happy. We had no time for each other, no time for ourselves, and no time for our new child on the way. I quit Marshall Field's and we moved down to Orlando, Florida: no job, no doctor, pregnant wife, and Goofus the dog. Stupid---me, not the dog. Okay, maybe both.

Brooke was born May 12, 1990. She is daddy's little girl--plays me like a fiddle and costs me a lot of money. I love her more than life itself. I know, more clichés. If you have kids, you know what I mean. She is smart, pretty, quickwitted, responsible, and impatient. Even as a teenager she has better judgement than me. I fall right behind her horse and the Internet in her order of affections. That's very high. Shortly after Brooke was born, I found a job in Orlando as a human resources manager for a hotel management company.

Slade was born in 1993. Man, is he good looking! Genetically, he is the best Lori and I can do. He is stubborn, funny, vain, kind, smart, offbeat, unfocused, sensitive, and loud. His room is a disaster area. He is a lot like me. We fight often, but, you got it, I love him more than life itself. I fall right behind any of his one thousand hot wheel cars in his order of affection. Oh, and his video games. Yes, that's very high.

When Slade was born, I was the Vice President of Human Resources and Quality for that hotel management company--an executive with responsibilities that included overseeing the PGA National Resort in Palm Beach Gardens,

Florida, the Lodge and Bath Club in Ponte Vedra Beach, the Buena Vista Palace Resort and Spa in Disney Village, and many more resort spas. A lot of people in my life thought this was the perfect job. Two years later I quit. Idiot.

After a couple of years starting up the Southeastern regional office for a human resources consulting firm, I committed myself to the Leadership Difference, an "enter-train-ment" company that I founded. Our mission is "Laugh and Learn!" Most of the next nearly ten years, which brings us to today, have exceeded all my preconceived notions of success. I have a family I love deeply, ample time to spend with my wife and children, a comfortable home, financial security, independence, and a carefree lifestyle. We moved to the mountains of Colorado where I hike a lot with Martini and Rossi (our two yellow labs, not the vermouth). We recently adopted Captain Morgan. Apparently, we are slowly accumulating a full canine liquor bar. Captain Morgan, or "Sparky" as we call him, is a kind soul with the wounded expression of someone who has witnessed great tragedy. Morgan survived Hurricane Katrina. Sadly, his owners did not.

Now you know a bit more about who you are dealing with. Keep in mind by the time this gets published, I might very well be running a wine store and doing volunteer work. Or not. Or part. Who knows? But one thing is for sure, it *has* been a life. It is a life that has held joy, heartache, anger, and angst--and that was just earlier today. Essentially, it is a life just like yours.

I will always remember something a friend, Dr. Steve Shealy, once said to me during one of my many moments of personal anguish: "Dave, act out of faith, not out of fear." Thanks, Steve.

Now, with a large amount of faith and a huge dose of fear, I present to you:

Live and Learn...or Die Stupid.

CHAPTER ONE

Be the Hand

INTERNAL LOCUS OF CONTROL

Being a speaker, trainer, and entertainer is an interesting profession. I spend a good deal of time loafing, at least when compared to my workload in the corporate world. Back then, I would work 50 to 60 hours a week and every moment I felt physically, mentally, and/or emotionally shackled to my job. Now, my cell door is open. Occasionally I have to step back inside: the conference call with a potential new client, talking with my accountant, filling out government paperwork, waiting out a travel delay. These are moments of incarceration. But for the most part, I loaf: sharing good times with my family, mountain biking and hiking, walking our dogs, listening to music, working out at the gym, reading, watching a movie, having a fine glass of wine, surfing the Internet. These are all examples of beautiful loafing for me.

Most of all, I love to spend time pondering. It has become my preferred loafing activity, alone or with a friend. I love to ponder, and I love to be paid to share my ponderings. This is my favorite thing: to amuse and lighten while I entertain and enlighten.

Often, after I speak, people come up to me and ask me whether I have a book. I have always been immensely flattered by this query. For the longest time I have said, "Oh, I'm just an average guy. Why in the world would you want to read a book that I wrote?" People have responded by saying how much they enjoyed listening to me, and how they would like to be able to revisit the concepts I presented when their memory of the event begins fading.

Consequently, after much hand wringing and self-talk, I have decided to write a book. This book will prove I am not a guru and, hopefully, establish more credibility for the concepts I have been offering. For me, it really isn't a book so much as it is a conversation between the two of us. The only thing, however, is I'm the one doing the talking, though in my mind I'm always remembering voices from hours of interactions with others (at least I'm hoping those voices in my head are from past conversations). What follows is a summation, of sorts, of all these previous conversations.

Okay, so we're just talking here, you and me. Let me ask you right off, do you think it is possible to be happy? I mean, really happy--not fake happy, not "I really have no reason to *not* be happy" or "I'm happy for the most part happy." I mean real contentment. I wonder. It seems to me that for a person to be consistently happy, content, and successful, he or she will need to possess certain characteristics. Maybe people just need some kind of a recipe or checklist for happiness.

Everything that is difficult in life--and I think "being happy" certainly qualifies as a challenge--starts with an instruction manual. This instruction manual, containing a checklist of characteristics of a happy person, is what

I have been pursuing my whole life. If we had such a list, we could develop our own little happiness curriculum around any characteristics that we don't currently possess. Or we could use the checklist to do diagnostic work when we are unhappy. Wouldn't that be cool? But what the heck would be on that checklist? Hmmm. I believe there is one fundamental attribute critical to our chances to be happy. Let's chat about that first.

"THEY WOULDN'T BE HAPPY IF YOU HUNG THEM WITH A NEW ROPE."

When I was 14-years-old, I started working for my dad each summer. He ran a little heating and air conditioning business in Greenup, Illinois. I would crawl around under houses or up in attics running duct-work to heat registers. Since he also sold and repaired appliances, I would also go along with him on deliveries or service calls. He paid me 25 cents an hour. (Did I mention that my father survived the Depression?) Anytime I would bring up my paltry compensation, I would be regaled for hours with stories of that era. Apparently my dad subsisted entirely on jam sandwiches ("That's two pieces of bread jammed together, Boy.") and entertained himself by riding a bicycle that he made himself. I never asked exactly how he managed this engineering feat for fear that I would be subjected to even more outrageous stories.

I was also responsible for keeping my dad's books. Now that I run my own business and have kids, I realize how questionable Dad's decision was to allow a 14-year-old to do his books. Anyway, while handling my dad's books, I began to realize some things about human nature. First of all, my father--a veteran of World War II, poverty, the Depression, and self -proclaimed "tough son of a bitch"--was a softie. With a struggling business his income was small, yet he always had a large amount of accounts receivable on the books. These were the people who had not yet paid Dad. Each month he would tell me to send out the statements, and each month I would dutifully go through these past due accounts and send out reminders. Over time, I knew who would actually pay and who wouldn't. Essentially, these accounts fell into four categories:

1. The people who had no money but would pay a little bit each month
2. The people who had no money and didn't pay at all
3. The people who had money but preferred to pay off their bill over time (since Dad didn't add interest)
4. The people who had money and didn't pay

My father had great admiration for the first group of people and continued to provide service for them, despite the fact that they owed him money. He groused quite a bit about the second group, but continued to provide them service when they needed it. ("Can't let 'em freeze to death, now can we, Boy?") Dad was most amused with the third group, often saying, "That's how they got rich."

For the final group my father had a special saying: "They wouldn't be happy if you hung them with a new rope." This he would say as he shook his head. My father had a lot of obtuse, vaguely violent little clichés like this. In fact, I am pretty sure that during my formative years, between the ages 12 and 16, my dad responded to every question I asked him with one of the following clichés:

> "I used to complain about my shoes until I met the man with no feet."

"Stand up for yourself or you'll be knocked down by someone else."

"Eat well 'cause it may be your last meal."

"No need to be depressed, things will get worse."

"Don't believe anything you hear and only half of what you see. But if it stinks, it stinks."

"I'm not gonna chew your ass out. I'm gonna chew around it and let it fall out!"

And, of course: "They wouldn't be happy if you hung them with a new rope."

"What does THAT mean?" I would ask.

"Bitchers and belly-achers," he would respond. "Those people wouldn't know a happy thought if it bit them in the butt. Call and ask them why they haven't paid, and they'll give you a hundred reasons. Add a service charge to their account, and every damn one of 'em will call me a crook."

"Why would they call you a crook when it is their fault that they haven't paid?" I responded with the naiveté of a 14-year-old.

"That's just it. They won't see it as their fault. They will think they are the victim and then refuse to pay out of principle. They'd complain about a sunny day because the bright light hurts their eyes."

I didn't know it then, but I just got my first memorable lesson in the concept of *internal locus of control*.

When your CTL container is full

Years later, as my eleven year career in corporate human resources management was grinding to a halt, I spent a good part of my day listening to employee grievances. Some were very legitimate and others were not.

After listening endlessly to both categories, I stopped trying to distinguish between the two. I was just plain burned out. I had become a very directive counselor. I now feel badly for those employees who came to me during this time.

"Hey, Bob. How can I help you today?" I would ask as the meeting began with an unhappy employee.

"Mr. Mitchell, I requested next Tuesday off and my manager denied the request," said the obviously troubled Bob.

"Then quit, Bob," and with that I would stand and escort Bob back to the door.

Bob seemed unsatisfied with my employee relations skills. Clearly, it was time for me to find a new line of work. My CTL container was full.

The CTL container, by the way, is a rarely discussed but tremendously important part of your neurological function. You won't read about it in medical journals, but I am here to tell you that many of life's conflicts and your personal anguish are both directly related to the status of your CTL container.

You look puzzled. Oh, you've never heard of the CTL container? Well then, you probably don't know what CTL stands for.

Crap Tolerance Level.

And when your CTL container overflows, it is ugly. I mean UGLY!

It wasn't that I didn't care. I just got worn out dealing with the people who always had a problem. As a result, after 11 years I was unable to muster the strength to find out which person had a legitimate concern and who was just a bitcher and bellyacher. Like I said, my CTL container was full.

Saddest part of all, I was becoming a bitcher and bellyacher, too.

I resigned and started my own company.

Today, I laugh when people commend me for the confidence to start my own company. Confidence had nothing to do with it. I couldn't get out of bed and go face that job in human resources one more day. I started my own company out of desperation, not confidence.

I had no clients, no capital, no office, no sales experience, no presentations, and no clue. And, as I discovered when I took back the bill-paying responsibilities from my wife (my lovely wife, who I adore, but who has a fondness for credit limits), I had more debt than money.

I was happy as a lark. I had just received an advanced lesson on the power of *internal locus of control*.

LIFE IS A BALLOON

Few people really have a plan. Oh, we can make our lives make sense with some creative revisionist history, but the fact of the matter is most of us aren't operating with a master strategy. However, I do take some pride in the fact that I have been willing to make adjustments in my life when I am not happy. I don't know how I come by this characteristic, but I am sure my father's relentless sharing of Depression-era stories had some influence. I realize now that this may have been the greatest gift my father gave to me. Consequently, it is a gift that I try to share. It is the gift of internal locus of control. Like many concepts, internal locus of control is most easily explained using a metaphor.

When I do keynote speeches I "invite" four members of my audience to join me on stage. I say invite, although the correct verb would probably be coerce. Maybe threaten. Or humiliate. Anyway, I manage to get four people up there with me. These four people and a balloon are all I need to provide a great example of locus of control. Try it yourself at your next party.

Line the four people up parallel to each other and about six feet apart. Tell them that you are going to tap the balloon to the first person, who will then tap it to the second person, who will tap it to the third person, who will tap it to the fourth person who will reverse the action until the balloon returns to the starter. Tell them that at no time is the balloon allowed to touch the floor.

The floor is *baaaad*.

Begin. It won't be hard. I have done this exercise hundreds of times with all kinds of people and only one time did they fail. I think it was a bad balloon. The experience won't necessarily be pretty. The balloon will go every which way, and people will be lurching in the most awkward ways as they use their hands and any other available body parts to try to guide the balloon back in the direction it needs to go.

Now, insert the word life for balloon in this experience and you've got yourself a metaphor for locus of control. (Or is it an analogy? Allegory? I never was sure about the correct usage of those words. I'm sure Mrs. Jackson, my high school English teacher, just released a sigh of resignation somewhere.) Anyway, let me explain.

Imagine if there were a sliding scale within each of us that represents our locus of control. On one side of the sliding scale is an internal locus of control and on the other side is an external locus of control. Where would your setting be on a consistent basis? Where you are on the scale has a lot to do with your level of happiness and success. You see, if your setting is over toward the external locus of control, then you are like the balloon in the exercise. That is to say, you are at the mercy of the hands that smack you.

Those hands are life events. Each time you are smacked by a life event, you have no choice but to travel in that direction.

People with an external locus of control have a hard time remaining happy. They can, however, tell you why they aren't happy: "My boss is a jerk"; "My job sucks"; "My spouse is an idiot, but we stay together for the kids. We want to make sure they are just as miserable as we are." These are the people that my father said would not be happy if you hung them with a new rope. They cannot achieve happiness because the key to their happiness exists outside of themselves.

This is exactly why so many of the people I counseled came back to my office again and again while I was a human resources manager. They were victims. Every time life got a little off track, they found something or someone else to blame. Unfortunately, toward the end of my career in corporate human resources, my own sliding scale of locus of control landed firmly on the external side as well.

People with an internal locus of control are like the hands that swat the balloon. They evaluate the developments in their lives and smack them in the direction they want their lives to go. It may not turn out exactly as they plan, but the fact that they take an active role in guiding their life means that it generally heads in the right direction. That is why I felt so much more happiness when I DECIDED, when I TOOK ACTION, when I walked out of the unhappy situation I was in while in the corporate world. Now, understand that I had been planning my business for a year, but it was more fantasy than reality. When I committed to a new life direction, I batted the balloon in the direction that I wanted it to go.

Now, reality check! I still have moments...days...even a week of unhappiness here and there. Slow business, bad luck, no mojo--I can end up in a funk for whatever reason. Knowing what it takes to be happy is a lot easier than executing it. I will tell you that there are a few things that can pull me out of these states. A paycheck in the mail always works like a charm. Someone might call and hire me; something randomly positive might occur like an email from a friend or a positive and reinforcing letter from a client; my mojo might mysteriously reappear (don't worry, we'll discuss mojo in chapter seven). All of these are frighteningly unpredictable. Or, I can sit down and decide what I need to do--what I NEED TO DO--to make things better. Inevitably, all it takes to begin feeling better is the latter. It just seems to take me a while to figure that out.

Looking back, many of the clichés my father shared with me involved this concept, "If you can change it, change it." That's a direct reference to using an ***internal locus of control***. "Do something, even if it's wrong." He always said this when he knew I was agonizing over a situation, or if I was bummed out because of boredom.

While I don't encourage people to be impulsive and perhaps multiply their troubles, I do think that inaction is far more dangerous than taking the wrong action. It seems as though it is easier to know what to do if you realize that what you are doing is wrong, than it is to sit around and do nothing besides try to figure out what's going on. I think it is kind of like the kid's game where a person hides something, then as the seekers search for the item, the person tells the seekers if they are getting warmer or colder depending on how close or far they are from the item. If there were another player who just stayed in one place and guessed where the item was, my bet is that he or she would take much longer to find the item. Maybe that's just me.

Another thing about locus of control, it's situational. By that I mean that a person can possess an internal locus of control about virtually every element of his or her life, but externalize control over just one thing, like a relationship with a parent, spouse, child, boss, colleague, or subordinate. I know when I start getting stressed out, it's usually a result of my feeling like a victim to something within my own life. So next time you are out of sorts, check to see if you have externalized the locus of control in some aspect of your life.

Not happy? What are you doing about it? People with an internal locus of control get bummed, too. It's just that they take action quickly to fix it. They are the hands, not the balloon. I don't believe that happy people have a great plan, or that they have been more fortunate than the rest of us. I believe their happiness has more to do with their *internal locus of control*. If life is a balloon…

Be the hand!

Oh, and on second thought, don't do that balloon exercise at your next party. You'll look like a dork.

CHAPTER TWO

My Own Private Idaho

TRANSITIONARY SPACE

You know, it occurs to me that before we go too far here I need to share my theory on reality. Actually, I doubt it is my own theory. I am sure many people, far brighter than I am, have written volumes on the nebulous nature of human reality. Of course, I do not read so I am unaware of this research. Well, to be fair, I do read some. While on airplanes I read *Esquire Magazine*. I also read *GQ, Details, Men's Health, Men's Fitness, The Sporting News, Wine Spectator, Wine Enthusiast, Sports Illustrated, Rolling Stone, Blender, Spin, MOJO, Men's Journal, No Depression* (it's about music, don't worry) and *New York Mets Inside Pitch*. Sometimes, when I am desperate for reading material, I will sink to *Psychology Today* or *Scientific American* or some such thing. They are kind of dry though. No celebrity pictures either.

Anyway, I do read, but not really what one might call "meaningful literature." So I am sure my theory on **transitionary space** is not new. But it was new to me, and as always, the result of obsessive pondering. Here's how I imagine human reality working. I believe that all of us human types who possess fully functioning (or as is the case with me and my eyeglasses, artificially corrected) sensory receptors (you know: eyes, ears, nose, mouth, nerve-endings), essentially have access to the same data that surrounds us. I call this entire database of information that is collectible by human sensory receptors **absolute human reality**. *Absolute human reality* is potentially the same for all people. To make this seem formal and important, I will repeat the definition in a separate font:

> *ABSOLUTE HUMAN REALITY* IS THE SUM TOTAL OF ALL DATA THAT CAN BE PERCEIVED BY HUMAN BEINGS USING THEIR SENSORY RECEPTORS: VISION, HEARING, SMELL, TASTE AND TOUCH. IT IS THE SAME FOR ALL HUMANS.

Of course, for us--and by us I mean all human beings--to experience the same *absolute human reality* we would all have to be standing in the same spot, facing the same direction, with the same acuity in all five senses, with...well, you get the idea. Obviously each individual's ability to experience *absolute human reality* is limited by his or her physical setting.

Additionally, I believe our sensory receptors are far better at collecting data than the cognitive function of the brain is at processing that data. In other words, we are immersed in far more gathered information than we actually choose to use. Basically, I believe we operate in spite of a serious design flaw. For human beings, input exceeds capacity to process. I mean, don't we all choose to only focus on certain things even though we are seeing or hearing much more? I know my wife has accused me of hearing the football score of the Minnesota Vikings amidst the swirling chaos of our household without hearing nary a word about my negligent household responsibilities. This is really just a self-preservation process to protect ourselves from being overwhelmed, or in my example above, to avoid doing the dishes and making coffee. Anyway, if we are collecting more data than we can process, then we must funnel, focus, and filter out certain information.

I consider the place within our minds where we select certain elements of *absolute human reality* and discard other elements to be our *transitionary space*. The end product of all this data collected from *absolute human reality* by our sensory receptors and shoved through our personal *transitionary space* is what I call ***individual interpreted reality***.

Individual interpreted reality is the unique life journey that each person experiences. It is what guides a person's actions, forms his or her opinions, and either contributes to or subtracts from his or her consistent happiness. It explains each person's behaviors. For the married women reading this book, this might explain some of your husband's behaviors. I mean, how many times have you reacted to your husband's behavior with, "Why in the world would you do that?"

The answer is, "They are not IN your world!" Your husband's behavior made perfect sense in his world. Going to Hooter's to celebrate your anniversary was totally logical. Food's good, game's on, beer's cold....come on!

Anyway, as my dad used to say, let me draw you a $%&@-ing picture. Dad came to profanity late in life and reveled in the rebellious nature of its use.

ABSOLUTE HUMAN REALITY

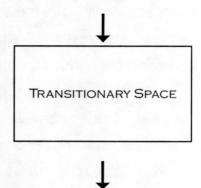

INDIVIDUAL INTERPRETED REALITY

So, if you assume (as I do) that each person constructs his or her individually interpreted reality with subsequent behaviors and happiness resulting from this construction, then one must examine the elements of the human condition that reside within transitionary space, since it is within transitionary space that **absolute human reality** (where everything is the same from human to human) is transformed into **individual interpreted reality** (where everything is unique to the individual).

Did anyone follow that? Whew! I think I have pretty much forfeited any chance of getting hired to write instructional manuals after that last paragraph.

Bottom line, I believe that there are some very important processes taking place within **transitionary space** that influence our happiness. Locus of control, from the last chapter, for instance, is one of these processes. The following chapters describe more. So, what should the reader take away from this discussion of how people construct reality? Probably a headache. But also, perhaps an appreciation that each of us has more influence over our life experience than we are conscious of. Perhaps by being more aware of how our approach to life influences our happiness, we can choose to do things that increase the quality of our life experience. Oh no, I'm beginning to sound like Tony Robbins. Not that there is anything wrong with Tony. He seems like a real confident guy. Walks on hot coals. Owns an island, I hear. Wow, I suck.

You know, let's just move on to self-loathing...er...I mean self-talk...the subject of our next chapter.

CHAPTER THREE

Buckaroo Banzai in Belize

POSITIVE SELF-TALK

I talk to myself.

You talk to yourself.

Everybody talks to themselves.

My wife talks to herself out loud, and when I catch her she says she is talking to our dogs (as if this were more reasonable).

I don't think there is anything more mysterious than our own brain. Our brain is so complicated that whole parts seem to work independently from one another. Performance psychologists talk about how positive visualization actually affects our physiology. In essence, our bodies are responding to an imagined scenario as if it were a real situation.

It makes perfect sense. I know I have conjured up negative imagery that resulted in a definite physiological response--a very unappealing response.

When I was in my early to mid-twenties, I worked hard to get established in the corporate world. I started my human resources career as a store trainer for Marshall Field's. I had no background in training and development and was (and still am) a bit of an introvert. While I knew I was a good and entertaining classroom instructor (a rare acknowledgement of my own value), I still felt a bit overwhelmed by other aspects of my job. Twelve to fourteen hour work days were the norm and each evening I would analyze upcoming challenges. This analysis would often have a negative tenor. I would worry about how to handle these situations and imagine that each challenge might be my demise.

Every three weeks or so I would experience intensely painful intestinal cramps.

I mean intensely painful.

I have had two kidney stones. They hurt. I mean, passing a rock through your...well, you get the picture. These intestinal cramps hurt even more.

I have had two children. Granted, the labor that accompanied their birth was far more painful for my wife than for me. Still, the pain I felt from my sense of helplessness while watching her labor was intense. The helplessness I felt from these intestinal cramps hit me even harder than the helplessness I experienced during Lori's labor.

I felt like that astronaut in the movie *Alien* who was the vessel from which the creature bursts forth. Each time it happened, I was pretty sure I was giving birth to an alien, and nothing gets your attention like giving birth to an alien.

The cramps would go on for hours and I would find myself lying on the floor of my bathroom, in the fetal position, praying for resolution. For three years I tried to draw correlations to certain foods. I monitored every possible variable I could think of. Finally, after three years of consistent, intermittent episodes of intense eye popping, excruciating pain, I decided to take extreme measures.

I went to a doctor.

Shocking.

Shocking for a man. After three years of pain and my wife's insistence, I yielded. I succumbed. I went to a doctor.

Seeing a doctor is very hard for many men. At 25-years-old I was not likely to receive the dreaded digital rectal exam, the most daunting deterrent to any visit to the doctor. In fact, at 25 I didn't even know what a digital rectal exam was. Now, at 44, I know. Maybe this is why I choose female doctors. Smaller digits.

What I did get to experience at 25 was the GI. I still don't know what that means. All I know is they have upper GIs, lower GIs, diagonal GIs, "bend over let me introduce you to a" GI. They have all sorts of GIs. I got to experience all of them and I am here to tell you, ain't none of them pleasant.

It's particularly confusing when a smiling doctor, barely able to contain his or her glee, tells you, "You're fine."

What?

Does that mean that everyone has excruciating abdominal cramps every three or four weeks? Ladies, put down your hands.

Okay, so roughly half of the population might have cramps like these, but I am not part of that demographic.

So, confirming what I had maintained all along, the visit to the doctor had accomplished nothing. Nothing except educate me on the humiliation of the GI procedure. Three weeks after my visit to the doctor I was back on the floor of my bathroom in the fetal position begging for resolution.

Back to the doctor. A different doctor. One with a different approach. No GIs. Hardly any discussion of my digestive tract at all. No, this doctor, an older man with a reassuring resemblance to Marcus Welby, asked me questions about my approach to life, not my diet. Then he said something that would change my life forever.

He told me my problem was in my head.

I hit him.

Okay, I didn't really hit him, but I've got to tell you, don't tell a Midwestern man, the product of an agricultural community, son of a Depression-era survivor, that he has a head problem. I bowed up. I went DeNiro on him. I said, "Oh no, Doc, I got pain. Pain YOU couldn't handle!"

"I know," he said, "and the origin of that pain is a result of how you are approaching your life mentally." He went on to explain that my body was responding to the mental stress to which it was being subjected, stress that I was creating: the endless analysis, negative speculation, and conjecture, the obsessing--all of these issues were creating an environment containing such duress that my intestines rebelled. Essentially, he summarized the psychology of all this with one sentence: "You have a third party relationship with yourself and that third party is way too critical."

In a nutshell, he explained, the way I was talking to myself was affecting my physical health and happiness. The cognitive function of my brain was influencing the autonomous function of my brain.

I was worrying myself sick.

Almost immediately the intestinal cramps started to subside. Now that I knew that they were self-inflicted I started to manage them. But that was just the tip of the iceberg. I began to realize how many other aspects of my emotional, mental, spiritual, and even (pause for effect) *physical* well-being were being affected by my negative self-talk. Of course, realizing something and changing something are two entirely different exercises.

Years passed before the next epiphany.

YOUR BEST FRIEND IS NOT ALWAYS THERE FOR YOU

Let me ask you this. Do you have a best friend? If you don't, lie. It is very depressing to admit to yourself that you don't have a best friend.

You may have more than one. I have two: my wife and Jerry Herships. My wife has shared virtually every important event in my life for the last 20 years. She has seen me at my best and my worst. Her devotion and support has always been unwavering. Her love is unconditional, as is my love for her.

Jerry is an entertainer and seminary student (It's complicated!) and the similarity in our vocations has provided the foundation of our relationship. We often work together. The shared experiences and the fact that we think alike, laugh about the same things, and have similar values have all helped forge our special bond.

My two best friends are not the same two that I have had my entire life. I have had two other best friends. Dennis Rodebaugh held the title from ages four to twenty-one. I lost track of Dennis over the years. I think of him a lot, but our lives have grown too far apart for us to be best friends. However, he recently came to visit and I remembered quickly why he had been my best childhood friend.

Scott Shafer has been akin to the utility infielder of best friends. He has always been in my life and every now and then steps back into the role. However, the distance between us and the passing of time has largely regulated Scott to the friendship bench. That's not a bad thing. It allows me the benefit of friendship "depth."

Anyway, my point is that I have two best friends. I bet most of you have at least one close friend. While it is unlikely that I know this person, I bet I can describe your relationship with him or her. You feel most comfortable with this person. You don't try to be something that you are not. You know that he or she loves you for who you are, warts and all. It is this comfort-level and unconditional love that makes the relationship so special. You may have grown up with this person, you may be related, you may even be married, but one thing is for sure: you love him or her simply for the person he or she is and vice-versa.

Well, let me tell you a few things about your best friend.

He or she is not always there for you.

He or she is probably not with you right now as you read this. He or she probably isn't with you at work. He or she isn't with you when you take your shower.

Not every shower. Okay, I'm guessing.

The fact is, no matter how close you are with your best friend, you will spend more of your life without that person than with him or her. You can marry this person or go into business with him or her, yet you will still experience more of life alone than with this person. There is only one person who will experience every life event with you. In other words, there is only one person who will always be there for you.

You.

You will spend your whole life with you. Because of this odd third party relationship between the cognitive you and the physical you, it is as if there are two distinct entities residing in your body.

You know what that means don't you? You better like you. You see, you can get rid of everybody else in your life. If you don't like your wife, divorce her. There are other fish in the sea. Kids are monsters? Give 'em up for adoption. Some loving family will take a chance on them. Boss is a jerk? Just walk into his or her office and say, "You know what (insert boss' name)? Later days and holidays!" Then turn and with your best cocky strut say, "Let me give you the last view of me you're ever gonna get."

For additional effect you can add some smack talk that I learned from my daughter, Brooke. Look your boss directly in the eye and recite, "Loser, loser, double loser, as if… whatever. Get the picture, duh?" To actually be effective you must accompany this smack talk with the corresponding choreography of hand gestures, head tilts, and swiveling hips. Ask any teenager to teach you.

You can get rid of everyone in your life if you don't like the way they treat you. You can get on a plane and fly to Belize. When you get to Belize, rent a bike. Ride that bike to the beach. Drop the bike and run. Run like the wind down that beach until you reach one of the most secluded spots in the entire world. There is not another human being within miles of you. But remember this.

"No matter where you go, there you are." (from *Buckaroo Banzai and the Adventures of the Eighth Dimension.* A great, obscure science-fiction movie.)

You can't run from you. To sum up, if you plan to achieve happiness, you better start with the relationship you have with yourself.

Having said that, most of us have a tenuous relationship at best with ourselves. If you are like me, you get tired of yourself. I mean, come on. Every single moment of every single day spent with me? I am 44 years old.

I don't think that's old, but it is the oldest I have ever been. Forty-four years spent entirely with myself. It is exhausting! Do you know we have never taken separate vacations! We haven't so much as had dinner apart during that time. Even when I try to take a quick break from me, boom, there I am. I get sick of me!

The worst moment often is first thing in the morning. You know what I mean? You get out of the bed and you go to the bathroom. And there's the mirror.

Who started that? Why is there a mirror in the bathroom? That is such a bad idea. Who was the freak that thought we needed a mirror to watch what happens in a bathroom?

Anyway, you start your day by catching a glimpse of yourself in the mirror. You stare at your image. This is definitely not the best you are going to look today. You stare and say to yourself, "Man, are you ugly!"

"But that's okay, cause you're fat, too"

"Fat and ugly. I'll just call you 'Fugly'. Fat and ugly."

There it is: your morning motivational speech. Could you imagine if your boss met you at the door of your employment each morning and said, "Hey, Fugly's here. Let's get to work, Fugly! Let's close some deals, FUGLY." That would be pretty hard to take. It certainly wouldn't be inspiring. It definitely wouldn't build self-esteem and confidence. But at least you could quit your job. Unfortunately, however, you can't leave *you*.

Now I am not suggesting that you get up each morning, lick your finger, place it on your hip, and listen for the sizzle as you look at yourself in the mirror and exclaim, "Oh, my God. You are sooo GORGEOUS!"

It may work for George Clooney, but it doesn't work for the rest of us.

My point is if each of us had the same relationship with ourselves as we do with our best friend, imagine how much happier we would be. Our best friend knows we are not perfect and they love us anyway. That's because they define us by our good qualities, not by our flaws. Oh sure, they support us as we try to improve and remind us when we fall short of our potential, but ultimately they love us unconditionally.

Human beings are not capable of perfection. If this is your goal, you are in for a lifetime of disappointment. The funny thing is that I have met some people in my time that appear to believe they have achieved perfection. They are annoying. The fact that they are annoying makes them imperfect. You see, perfection is impossible.

I remember coming home from school when I was 16-years-old. I was bummed because the most spectacular girl in school, who I dug like a ditch, wouldn't spit on the best part of me. The pain of our unrequited love radiated through my entire being such that even my dad, with his limited emotional sensitivity, could see that I was depressed.

"What's wrong with you?" Dad asked.

Hesitantly, I offered the reason from my morose state. "There's this girl at school that I really, really like but she doesn't like me. I think it's my nose." I have one of those long, thin Romanesque-sort-of-noses that look fabulous on Matt Lauer and Adrian Brody. I didn't like it on me.

"Yeah, you got a big nose," Dad said in a matter of fact way.

It was at this moment that I realized that my nurturing needs in life would be fulfilled by people other than my father.

Dad quickly realized that his response had not brightened my spirits. "Well, I mean, Son, your nose is right there on your face so we've all seen it. What makes you think this girl doesn't like you because of your nose?"

"Well, sometimes kids have pointed out that I have a big nose, so I just assume if this girl doesn't like me, it's cause of my nose."

And then Dad offered what appeared to be an early indication of dementia. "Listen, the only kids pointing out your nose are the ones with big ears."

cricket sounds

"What?"

"Son, everyone has flaws. Some flaws you can see, others you can't-- and thems the ones you should worry about. Anyway, if someone is pointing out your flaws, it's because they don't want anyone seeing theirs. That's all. And if that girl don't like you for something as stupid as the size of your nose, then she ain't worth ruining your day over."

I tell you, I heard what my dad said and immediately--within 10 years--I got it. Like most 16-year-olds, I was somewhat slow on the uptake. But eventually I realized that we all magnify our own imperfections because we are so doggone familiar with them. The key is not the fact that we have flaws. Our gifts are the key.

How do you nurture the relationship you have with yourself? I think you start by listening to your self-talk. Do you talk to yourself the way you would expect your best friend to talk to you? Do you define yourself by your positive qualities while striving to be the best person you can be? I think that's the goal.

Positive self-talk.

By the way, my dad ended our little counseling session with this nugget, "And, by the way, ain't nothing wrong with your nose."

I remember feeling like my dad had told me he loved me for the very first time. A few years later I would meet Lori. She loves my nose. Dad was right.

Chapter Four

Hats in the Highway

Positive focus

I must admit that I am a bit cynical. I don't read self-help books because I tend to dismiss their advice as overly-simple and Pollyanna-ish. As a result, it makes perfect sense that I would write a book that examines the personal characteristics that promote a happy and contented life using research culled only from my musings. Perhaps that is why I have struggled to write this book for so long.

One example of my misguided disdain for self-help literature revolves around *The Power of Positive Thinking* by Norman Vincent Peale--an undisputable classic in providing a framework for a happier existence written by a hugely intelligent and insightful spiritual leader. I, of course, dismissed it as syrupy optimism after having read it in my mid-30s. It would be several years later when the memories of my first child's birth and a friend's baseball hat collection would lead me to rethink the impact one's perspective has on one's life.

BABIES ARE LAZY

My wife and I made a decision to wait five years after we were wed before we started a family. It is probably the only example of a plan we have ever had during our marriage. We generally...no, we are always impulsive in our major life decisions. So the fact that we decided to wait five years to have our first child and actually made it four and a half years is the best example we can offer for having a plan. Therefore Brooke, our daughter and first-born, was planned.

As is so often the case with first-time parents, we read every book about parenthood and pregnancy. We gleefully prepared for the new arrival, painting and purchasing and outfitting and generally engaging in the rampant materialism that accompanies the birth of a child. Entire evenings and social gatherings would revolve around a shift or a kick by the baby. We would invite family, friends, UPS delivery people, and street musicians to feel my wife's stomach. We learned the language of the fertile: trimester, contraction, Lamaze, and sonogram.

Nine months of unbridled anticipation came to fruition on May 12, 1990, when my wife gave birth to our baby girl. Then, when we brought our bundle of joy home, I was overwhelmed with one singular feeling.

Disappointment.

Yep.

Babies are lazy.

Brooke was a healthy, normal, beautiful baby. Healthy, normal, beautiful babies don't do much. They don't engage you in interesting conversation. They don't generate revenue for the household. They don't help with chores. And they don't play catch.

That is when I realized my desire for fatherhood, planned as it might have been, was rooted in a desire to have someone to play catch with. Brooke, the baby, didn't play catch. Heck, she didn't even walk! In fact, she not only didn't walk, but she showed no interest in walking. How could this be, I asked myself? Walking would be so useful to her, especially until she gets a driver's license.

That's when I started reading Herzog.

I probably picked up the book thinking it was the memoirs of Whitey Herzog, the major league baseball manager.

But this Herzog was an educational theorist. I was already hooked before I realized this guy wasn't talking baseball. When I read Herzog's theory about the steps involved in learning, I realized that Brooke's situation went *beyond* not knowing how to walk. Brooke suffered from what Herzog referred to as unconscious incompetence.

She didn't know she didn't know how to walk. My daughter was clueless.

Soon Brooke became aware she didn't know how to walk. You could see her eyes follow you as you moved swiftly around the room while upright on your legs. You could tell she was curious about this fascinating skill.

At that point she had moved to Herzog's next level of learning: conscious incompetence. Arguably the most important step, Brooke had identified a skill that existed but that she did not possess, which would now allow her to go about learning that skill. She now knew she didn't know how to walk. In other words, she had gone from clueless to stupid.

Within months she had moved to <u>conscious competence</u> (she knew that she knew how to walk). You know, the stage during which the child selects the sharpest, most dangerous piece of furniture in your home and tries to walk toward it. The child teeters and staggers while steadily moving closer and closer to the corner of the coffee table that is exactly the same height as their right eye. She had gone from clueless to stupid to awkward.

Anyway, reaching this third stage is critical to expanding one's mind and skills. Or becoming a pirate named Lefty.

I feel compelled to offer an aside here to all you new and future parents: Why is it that we adults feel it necessary to assist our young toddlers in their quest to walk by grabbing their arms and holding them over their head? The only devices at their disposal to help them maintain balance--the arms--and we, the trusted caregivers, render them useless. I am convinced that all children would be walking at four months if their parents would stay out of the experience.

Now, back to Brooke. She would eventually become so adept at walking that she qualified as being <u>unconsciously competent</u>. She, like most of us, no longer had to think about walking. This is the state that most of us experience when we are walking--unless you close the local bar on a Saturday night, in which case you slide back to the conscious competence stage. Or sometimes just the unconscious stage--ba-da-boom! (Pause for reader to get the joke or reread as necessary.)

Brooke had moved from clueless to stupid to awkward to skilled.

While watching my daughter work her way through these steps, I was simultaneously experiencing one of my infrequent but life-altering epiphanies.

How much information exists in the world that I am completely unaware of? An even deeper thought followed that question: How much information exists in the world that I am incapable of being aware of?

Scooby-Doo moment....aaahuuuhh?

THERE IS NO REALITY

Like all human beings, I am self-centered. Unless you are Shirley MacLaine and have frequent-out-of body experiences, most of us spend our entire lives with one distinct point of view, our own. This point-of-view is limited by our own biomechanics. As fully functional human beings, we are capable of collecting data about reality using five sensory receptors: vision, hearing, smell, taste, and touch. In fact, we talked about this earlier when we discussed *individual interpreted reality*. We know, scientifically, that there are data, substances, entities, et cetera that we are unable to collect based on our biomechanical limitations. Therefore, some of this information is collected through scientific means (microscopes, Geiger counters, gas detectors, et al.) because at some point we were able to reach conscious incompetence and design technology to help us detect and understand things we were becoming aware of, but had little knowledge about.

What about the information that resides in that area of unconscious incompetence? I imagine that there is nearly an infinite amount of information about which we are clueless. Judging by the rapidity of change in the modern world, we have just scratched the surface of what we can know as human beings. That doesn't even speak to all the information we are just not capable of understanding due to the limitations of the human condition. Bottom line, the *absolute human reality* that I defined earlier is a tiny subset of all things that exist.

Whoa!

So for me, watching my daughter learn to walk became an exercise in quantum physics, biomechanics, and existential philosophy. (My wife says I think too much. I wonder what she means by that?)

What does this have to do with happiness? Well, I'm getting there. We still have to talk about baseball hats. Suffice it to say, when you realize that the version of reality you are working with is actually a subset of all that is real, that can give you pause for thought. It opens up the possibility of alternative realities. That said, you may well be wondering (or pondering), what good are alternative realities when they reside beyond the scope of the human condition? Good question, and that is where the story about baseball hats get introduced.

IT MUST BE SOME ODD STATE LAW IN TEXAS

I have a friend who is a behavioral psychologist. Actually, I have two friends who are psychologists. The fact that pyschologists keep entering my life randomly may be a compelling hint from the universe about my need for therapy! Anyway, they are both odd--not in a weird way, but in that endearing, eccentric way. The two of them provide great fodder for conversation, both because of their knowledge *and* their behavior.

Tom, one of these friends, lives in Texas. He collects baseball hats-- major league baseball hats. Because he was aware of my love of the game (I played organized baseball until the age of 20 and would later be revered as a successful coach at the tee-ball level), Tom felt that I would appreciate his collection of hats. I didn't have the heart to tell Tom that my love of baseball had very little to do with the apparel. On one of my trips to Texas, Tom invited me to his home to view his collection. As I stepped through the French doors and entered his den, I was surrounded by 125 major league baseball hats on display.

I don't think I could effectively paint a mental image for you of the enormity of a 125 major league baseball hat collection. But despite its enormity, it was not the size of the collection that was so awe-inspiring. It was the actual condition of these hats.

These were the nastiest, gnarliest hats I had ever seen. I mean, having played baseball I know how superstitious baseball players can be. When they go on a hitting streak, they don't change any articles of clothing, least of all their hats. But I am telling you, you cannot do what had been done to these hats on the baseball diamond. As I stood there in that doorway, dumbfounded, I tried to work up all the tact and diplomacy that my 11 years of corporate human resources training had afforded me before I turned to Tom.

"Dude, what's up with these hats? They are ugly!"

Yet another example of why I was not cut out for the corporate world.

"Oh, I forgot to tell you how I come by these hats," Tom replied. "I don't buy them. They are not given to me. I find them. I pick them up on interstate highways while riding my motorcycle."

Silence.

I remember thinking to myself, How long have I known Tom? How did I end up here in his home, alone? Does anyone know I am here?

Finally, I broke the awkward moment. "So, you found these hats on the road?"

"No, not roads. Not city streets or U.S. highways. It has to be an Interstate," corrected Tom. "And I have to be on my motorcycle." Tom was becoming increasingly manic.

"How long you been doing this, Tom?"

"About three years."

"THREE YEARS! And you have found 125 hats?"

"Well, probably more like 150, but a few have been so beat up that my wife wouldn't let me keep them."

Based on the condition of the "keepers," I imagined what the 25 rejects must have looked like. I also speculated on my wife's reaction to me collecting beat-up baseball hats and quickly realized that Tom's wife was either a saint or catatonic. Or both. Then it hit me.

This man had found an average of one major league baseball hat each week for the last three years while riding his motorcycle on interstate highways.

I could not recall seeing any hats on any road while riding in or on any vehicle in the entire 36 years that I had been on the planet up to that time. Yet this man was finding one hat a week of a specific type on a specific roadway while riding a specific vehicle.

I HAVE seen some shoes in the road.

Weird. Always a big clunky work-boot. Left foot. What's up with that? Are certain people driving to work with their window down and a boot just blows off their left foot? "Damn, I just lost my boot!"

Anyway, here I was, 36 years old with no hats. Then things got even more strange. That weekend, Tom took me to Galveston. It's about a two-hour drive to Galveston from Tom's house. On the way, he pointed out three hats. We weren't on an interstate highway, nor were we on his motorcycle, so we didn't stop to determine if they were major league baseball hats. But the fact that the man could point out three hats on the road to me in two hours, after I had gone 36 years without seeing one, was freaking me out.

Initially I figured it must be a Texas thang. I speculated that Texas must have some odd state law that requires that its residents celebrate each new day by flinging a hat out the window of their car. "Yeehaw, it's Wednesday!" I don't know; I've never lived in Texas.

When I returned home to Orlando, what do you think I saw?

Hats. Everywhere.

It was like an X-Files episode. You go your whole life without seeing a hat in the road and then someone comes up to you and says, "Oh, they're out there," and boom, there they are. Now I was really freaking out!

What's that about?

So I did a little research. That's generally how thorough I am. I do a little research, a little more observation, and a lot of pondering. I prefer to spend endless hours theorizing and hypothesizing on issues that have long ago been completely fleshed-out, meaning the mental mystery in which I am immersed is only a Google away from being solved. As a result, based on a smattering of actual science, here's what I think is going on here.

Our brains are struggling to make things simple enough for our mind to comprehend. This means that within our *transitionary space*, collected data is filtered for familiar information. We, in fact, have filters that ensure we notice (and place in our individual interpreted reality) information that is important to us. Some of this activity is done consciously; some of it is not.

We can see a lot more information than we can effectively process. In other words, the brain can collect far more visual information than the mind can process. As a result, we choose a focus. This can be a very conscious act. This focus now defines our visual information. For example, as a public speaker, when I look into my audience, I can choose the faces on which I will focus. If I choose to focus on someone who is smiling and nodding and laughing, then I will feel encouraged because my visual information seems to indicate that I am doing a great job. If I choose to focus on someone who has a furrowed brow and a scowl on their face, I will feel self-conscious and think I am not doing well.

Note to self and other speakers: The smiling, nodding, laughing person may be thinking, "What an idiot!" while the person scowling may be thinking, "This is the best information I have heard in my life!" You never know. That's why it's called individual INTERPRETED reality.

The fact is that I am changing my reality by what I choose to focus on. For further study on this subject, please reread Chapter Two, My Own Private Idaho, which introduces **individual interpreted reality** in this very book. (I know, I don't like to actually get up from the couch to do research, so I figured I would just reference my own book. Sweet, huh?)

It doesn't end there. In addition to the focus that you choose, there are also filters of which you are less conscious. Filters are little files that your brain sets up to protect you in the event that you choose the wrong focus. Let me give you an example. I love sports. If I am walking around the planet and sports information enters my field of view (swoosh), I will immediately notice it regardless of my current focus. I love music. Should music information enter my field of view, my brain will immediately (swoosh) change my focus to the music. I also love wine. When information about good wine enters my field of view, I will notice it. (Did I mention I am a certified sommelier? No real reason to mention that except for my need to brag about it, and my wanting you to understand a bit more about my love of wines.) I have other filters as well, but I am not going to share them all with you. You have a lot of filters, too.

The end result of all this is that our view of reality at any given time is largely determined by our focus and filters. For example, there are no two people closer than Lori and I are to one another. We have been together for nearly half of our lives, know each others' thoughts, and have many shared experiences. Yet when we go to the mall, despite the fact that we can be side-by-side, hand-in-hand, we are *not* in the same mall. My mall is comprised of music stores and sporting goods stores. Her mall is one big shoe store. Different focuses and different filters.

Tom had a baseball hat filter. For a couple of weeks, so did I. I dumped mine. I don't want to see hats in the road.

Having experienced the power of focus and filters, I now had a new perspective on Normal Vincent Peale's book. What at one time appeared to be misguided optimism and Pollyanna-ism, could now be viewed as choosing a positive focus. I realized that to choose to define reality in negative terms was not only self-destructive, but downright stupid. Who the heck wants to live in a world full of problems, barriers, and enemies, when a person can just as easily choose to live in a world of opportunity, resources, and friends?

I also began to better understand those people who constantly complained. I had wasted my time and theirs trying to impose my focus on them. My version of the world was accurate, but so was their version. That's why they seemed stubborn. They weren't stubborn, they were right. And so was I. The difference was that we each chose to focus on different elements of our world. I saw more of the good; they saw more of the bad.

Oh, don't get me wrong. I know there is evil in the world. I know bad things happen. The point is, how we choose to define the world and the people and the situations around us determines whether the world seems good or bad. **Absolute human reality** is neither good or bad--it is **individual interpreted reality** that takes on this dimension. Do we look for what is wrong or do we look for what is right? People who choose a positive focus have much less stress in their lives. People who choose a positive focus have an easier time being happy on a more consistent basis.

The choice seems clear...a positive focus. We are all delusional. Why not create a good delusion?

CHAPTER FIVE

Stunned by the Lollipop Guild

PROMOTE *SEAMWORK*

It had been quite a week.

Seven years ago my career as a public speaker/enter-trainer was chugging along at less than a breakneck pace. Although it was supporting us and I was pleased, I was still in a general state of anxiety about our future most of the time. But there was one week that was the most incredible week of my professional career.

On Monday I was in Basking Ridge, New Jersey doing some work for AT&T. On Tuesday, I was in Michigan speaking to General Electric. On Wednesday, I was in Virginia in front of the CIA. (Okay, so it was the human resources department, but it is still cool to say that I was speaking to the CIA. I remember being very apprehensive about that gig. What happens if they are not satisfied? I have heard stories.)

Each of the above clients had hired me to do a team-building event. During each of these events I used an exercise I creatively referred to as the rope exercise. I called it this because it involved a rope. Brilliant!

The exercise involved me taking out a rope and laying it out in front of the classroom. Then I would take two members of the audience who worked in the same department and put them at one end of the rope. Next I would take two other members of the audience who also worked together but in a different department than the first two people, and I would place them at the other end of the rope. I would then tell the first pair that for them to win they would have to get the other pair at the opposite end of the rope on their side of the room. Next, I would turn to the other team and explain that for them to win they must do the same: get the first pair at the opposite end of the rope on their side of the room. Essentially, I had set up a corporate game of tug of war.

Then I would say, "GO!"

Oh, the humanity of it all.

I would watch as four intelligent corporate leaders, some dressed in Hugo Boss and Donna Karan, pulled with all their might against each other.

Note to self: generally only sales executives were dressed in designer labels. Operations executives were often dressed in less flashy apparel. Just another example of "the man" keeping us operations people down.

Images of personal injury lawsuits would flash through my head as I witnessed the force with which the participants pulled. The four executives, straining under the effort to achieve victory, would ultimately wind up with the worst of all results. The dreaded tie. No winners.

At every organization it was the same result: tremendous effort, no advantage. I would go into more detail but I still fear reprisal from the CIA.

That was my week...until Friday. Friday changed everything.

It was the Friday gig that was the most incredible. Friday involved the Lollipop Guild.

Well, not the original guild, not the ones from *The Wizard of Oz*, but a group that was virtually identical. This guild was the Orlando Astros: fourteen kids--four, five, and six-years-old--assembled to play tee-ball. I was their coach, their mentor, their guide through the journey of baseball. Friday was our first ever practice--our first steps along this wondrous path. Clearly, I was psyched.

I volunteered to coach tee-ball because I wanted to get more involved in my community. Since I generally get upset when exposed to people who are suffering physical pain, emotional duress, or economic crisis; and since I am not particularly good at fundraising, administration, or project management, my options for community service are significantly limited. My two options at that time were picking up roadside trash or coaching baseball. Picking up trash did have a certain attraction, but I know baseball, I told myself, and I am an educator of sorts, so youth baseball seemed to be my niche.

My first official act as "Coach Mitchell" was to construct my objectives for the season. As I walked onto that baseball field at 5:00 P.M. that Friday in March 1999, the Central Florida sun slowly making its way toward the horizon, I mentally reviewed my vision for the season. Ah, yes, the Orlando Astros, these exuberant, earnest and dedicated future leaders would learn, from me, the beauty of our national past-time. We would explore the strategies and tactics that make baseball the most cerebral and intricate of all sports. We would examine the subtleties and nuances hidden beneath the surface of the game. Most importantly, we would discover the life lessons that play out between those two chalk lines: the metaphors and analogies for success that translate into the intangible that will serve these youngsters for a lifetime, all shared by a sage educator of savvy adults.

I would be molding minds.

That was my vision at 5:00 P.M....

...by 5:20 P.M. I had changed my goals. My new purpose was more singular and pure. My new vision was to return 14 children to their parents promptly at 6:00 P.M. I didn't even care if the parent received the same child they had dropped off. To me, my responsibility was the accuracy of the numbers.

"Here you go, Mrs. Khoury. Bobby had a great practice."

"Hey, this isn't Bobby!" responds a disconcerted Mrs. Khoury.

"Just take him. This kid is better looking than Bobby anyway. You traded up."

By 5:40 P.M. a horrifying realization had descended upon me like a famished vulture plucking the carcass of a dead opossum. (I tend to become a drama queen in times of personal duress.) I had run out of things to do. I had run out of things to do a full 20 minutes before practice was over! I had to fill 20 more minutes of time with these "baseball players" before I could hand them back to their parents. TWENTY MINUTES! Could we run the bases for 20 minutes? Unlikely. Could I bear to watch them attempt to catch, throw, or hit for another 20 minutes? Certainly not. Could I end practice 20 minutes early? Are you kidding me? Those parents won't be back for their kids one second before 6:00 P.M.! I racked my brain for something, anything to entertain these kids. Then it hit me.

In the back of my car was the rope.

Lots of applications for that rope went through my mind.

Many involved Bobby Khoury.

But I made the right choice. I spread the rope out behind the pitcher's mound and in front of second base and I waved all my little sluggers into the infield. As 28 eyes watched me intently, I explained the rules of this game we were about to play. Just like I had done at AT&T, General Electric, the CIA, and countless other corporate institutions, I pitted two teams of two kids against each other on opposing sides of that rope. I explained to each team that they would need to get the other team on their side of the rope to win. Just as I had done hundreds of times before, I yelled, "GO!" and waited for the stalemate.

The stalemate never happened.

They switched sides.

It took them about seven seconds. I think six seconds were spent on them trying to convince themselves there must be more to this game than that.

As I stood there with my lower jaw grazing the infield dirt in disbelief, those four kids, with only a moments hesitation, switched sides. Now, they stood staring at me with a look of overwhelming boredom until Bobby Khoury said, "Do you have any other games, Coach? That one's kinda lame."

Right then it hit me. I wasn't going to teach these kids about baseball. Heck, no. They were going to teach me. They were going to teach me about baseball and about life. I thought I knew baseball. I didn't know baseball. I didn't know that the baseball glove is perfectly designed for the transport of dirt from third base to second base. They taught me that.

I didn't know the importance of the dandelion to the game of baseball. If a dandelion, with all its seeds intact, exists anywhere on the field, it must be personally inspected by each player and then the seeds must be ceremoniously blown into the wind. Until this takes place, no other action can occur on the playing field.

I didn't know how important it was to celebrate. Oh sure, if you come back from a huge deficit, win the pennant with a "walk-off" home-run, beat the favored team in extra innings, knock yourself out celebrating. But these kids taught me a whole new criterion for celebrations. In the unlikely event that an opposing player should happen to hit a ball in fair territory, that is such cause for raucous and joyous celebration that each and every player on our team must chase after that ball and attempt to touch it; even if it means tackling your own teammate to do this. This, of course, causes a 15-minute delay in action while I meticulously replace all the players in their defensive positions.

By the way, there are no conventional baseball positions in tee-ball. No first baseman, second baseman, third baseman, shortstop or the like. Nay, nay, Nelly. In tee-ball, there are flight patterns. You study the most likely paths that a batted ball will travel and you place as many players as possible in the way of this path. Then, when the ball strikes one of your players, you yell, "Nice stop, Billy. Stop crying and throw the ball to first!"

I didn't know about the language of the game, either. Oh, I thought I did. I watch Sportscenter on ESPN. I stay up on the current jargon of the game. I pride myself in my knowledge of the latest and coolest home-run calls and street slang. Yet, clearly I did not know the language of this game. That became clear during our first game of the season.

Now, you need to know that I am an aggressive coach, particularly when it comes to base-running strategy. I believe that you put pressure on the opposing team's defense to make the play. Until the other team shows they can perform in the field effectively, you keep taking the extra base. Well, we played the Orioles in our first game and I had cast a keen eye upon their defensive execution. I found their play lacking. It was then I decided to become aggressive on the base paths.

I coached third. I coached third because I like to be involved in the game--a critical on-field decision maker influencing the action in the moment. I also coached third because I could only get one other parent to help me with the team and he coached first, but that is beside the point. Anyway, we were batting and Bobby Khoury was on second base. Bobby was a fleet-footed five-year-old with good instincts. I knew, based on my painstaking observations and scouting of the Orioles defense, that he could score on a ball hit just about anywhere in the field. I yelled out to Bobby to be alert. He immediately stopped playing in the dirt around second base and looked around for some reason to actually be alert.

Then it happened. The ball was hit slowly to the right side of the infield. I knew immediately that Bobby could score on this slow-roller. As if shot out of a cannon, Bobby came toward me. Without hesitation, calling upon my many years of baseball experience, I screamed, "GO HOME!"

He left.

It turns out that Bobby Khoury lived three blocks from the ballpark. He sprinted the entire way to his house. While I was disappointed in our miscommunication, I took a special delight in seeing him hustle. That, to me, was evidence of good coaching.

I spent 45 minutes on the phone with his mother explaining that he had not been kicked off the team. I wondered if Joe Torre ever faced these types of dilemmas with players.

These kids also taught me about life. They loved to play. They rooted for each other. They even rooted for the other team. They weren't competing so much as they were having fun and doing the best they could. That's why they didn't pull against each other in the rope exercise. It never dawned on them that they were competing. I had explained what they needed to achieve to win and they immediately recognized that each team's objectives could be accomplished simultaneously. In the words of Stephen Covey, they created a win-win situation. Now, I don't know what kids today are reading in kindergarten, but I find it hard to believe that Covey's *Seven Habits of Highly Effective People* would be on their list.

That was my epiphany.

Somehow between the ages of six-years-old and adulthood we forget something. I have been hired numerous times to build teamwork. I think these events have merit and my family certainly appreciates the income derived by my efforts to help companies enhance teamwork. But lately I have been re-evaluating the value of teamwork. With the rugged economic environment that accompanied the new millennium, most of the ineffectual teams were fired or restructured. Effective teamwork became widespread due to this Darwinian effect. The problem isn't teamwork.

The problem is **seamwork**. Seamwork is something that my Orlando Astros understood inherently and that most adults simply do not. Seamwork is different from teamwork. Seamwork is the ability to cooperate despite the boundaries that separate you. Seamwork stretches beyond departmental lines, divisional organizational charts, and borders on a map. Seamwork succeeds in the midst of differences.

To illustrate this, think of a patchwork quilt. Each little piece of fabric within the quilt is strong. Each piece is beautiful, unique, and SMALL. It cannot accomplish much of great importance because of its diminutive size. However, when these pieces of fabric are sewn together they make a quilt.

A quilt can accomplish so much more. The effectiveness, the strength of this quilt, will be largely the result of the quality of the seams.

It is the same in the corporate world. The vast majority of companies that I have worked with have excellent teamwork within the individual departments of the organization. The problems are far more likely to be in the seams, those areas where the different departments are linked. It is in the seams of an organization that the company feels the impact of the rope exercise-- for instance, sales pulling against operations and vice versa. Corporations compete against themselves far more often than they compete against their competition.

The same can be said with our communities, perhaps even our world. We operate under the assumption that to allow another to win automatically makes us lose. But helping others win doesn't make you a loser. Quite the opposite. Think about how you feel when someone wins at your expense. You immediately want the chance to "get even". Winning at someone else's expense would lead to being surrounded by losers who are consumed by the desire to get even with you. This kind of winning is not sustainable.

Conversely, creating winners all around you insures you will be surrounded by people who want nothing more than to help you succeed. That's what those kids taught me: focusing on what you can do to contribute to the success of others is the best way to insure success for yourself. That is the concept of **seamwork** in a nutshell.

Now, I remind you that I spent a great deal of time in the corporate world and I saw my share of rising stars who stepped on the heads of their colleagues to reach greater success. But looking back, I don't remember any who could maintain that success. In the words of one of my favorite philosophers, Lowell George, the lead singer of *Little Feat*: "The same dudes you abuse on the way up, you will meet up with on the way down." (From the song "On the Way Down," by Allen Toussaint, off the album *Dixie Chicken*, Warner Brothers Records, 1973, side 1/track 4.) Music is one of my filters, remember?

My brother-in-law, Russ, who should have been born during the time of the great philosophers like Plato or Socrates, once said, "Dave, I think when a man dies, if the people that he knew in life remember him with kind thoughts, then that person is in heaven. And if they remember him as a son-of-a-bitch, well then, he is in hell." The fact that Russ was liquored up at the time does not diminish the genius of that simple insight.

Maybe the key to heaven's gate is promoting **seamwork**. Certainly, a large component of personal happiness is postively sewing yourself into the fabric of the lives of others.

CHAPTER SIX

Carl Jung and the Muppets

UNDERSTANDING HUMAN BEHAVIOR

After college I worked briefly for the CBS television network. While that may sound impressive to some, it is worth noting that the station I worked at was in Terre Haute, Indiana. Now, before I have an entire city of Larry Bird loyalists screaming obscenities at me, please understand that I respect Terre Haute. The rather pungent odors of the Wabash River aside, Terre Haute was a major improvement in culture for a young man raised in Greenup, Illinois. I have nothing but the highest regard for the city and have often ordered my compact discs from this record club capital of the world. How can someone who loves music not hold a special place in his heart for a city that serves as the headquarters for a company that will send him 11 CDs for just a penny? Still, having since been exposed to many other cities in the world, Terre Haute has moved rather significantly down my personal list of favorite destinations. But, I digress.

As it turned out, broadcast journalism wasn't my cup of tea and I left this job to embark on a journey of self-discovery. Two months into my journey, I discovered myself behind the photo-development counter at a local Osco Drug store wearing a ratty company issued smock and placing price tags on cosmetic products. It wasn't quite what I had envisioned. Chicks didn't dig it either.

A couple of other dead-end jobs followed. The most memorable of this otherwise completely forgettable period of my career was my job as a videographer for a "talent agency" that traveled from town to town. Their advertisements said they could help get people on *Star Search* by providing them with an audition tape that highlighted their "talent." I use the quotation marks because much of the "talent" that was uncovered by the "talent agency" involved adult dance routines (read "strippers"). While that might sound like a pretty sweet gig for a 22-year-old boy/man, my rural Midwestern upbringing ensured that my modesty, naiveté, and general discomfort with this dynamic would preclude any possibility of enjoyment.

My rigid and repressed upbringing, combined with the requirement to occasionally work as a canvasser for the owner's other business, an aluminum-siding company, ended my brief stint in the "talent" discovery field. For those who may not be familiar with the term "canvasser," this is the person who goes door to door in a neighborhood and tries to tactfully convince people that their otherwise fabulous but ugly house would benefit by having aluminum-siding installed. While I certainly could see the value, I had no aptitude for this type of work. On top of that, I was troubled by the premise that owning an aluminum-siding company qualified a person to run a talent agency.

I also had no aptitude or interest in my dad's heating and air conditioning business. Of course every time my next new job became my next ex-job, I would land back under a house or in an attic installing ductwork for Dad's business. Each time I returned, I would think perhaps I could be happy running the family business. About three days later I would remember why I couldn't be happy doing Dad's business for long. It was a nagging combination of no aptitude and no desire to install ductwork for a living.

Eventually, I found myself entertaining the idea of traveling across the country with a friend of mine, who convinced me (or I convinced him, I can't recall) that we could finance this Kerouac-like adventure by doing odd jobs in each town we would temporarily call base. I am not sure how we came up with this plan, but I do know it seemed more exciting and reasonable when we engaged in the consumption of substances that altered our judgment.

Helpful tip: it is probably a good indication of the viability (or lack thereof) of a life strategy if you find that it seems more exciting and reasonable when you are under the influence of something that is not available in a drug store, even if it can be purchased from a slightly shady stock person from the back of the drug store's loading dock.

Anyway, somehow my sister got wind of this newest development in my career planning and intervened. My sister, being 17 years older than I am and a master's level guidance counselor, felt perhaps there might be some other options worth exploring before choosing the Kerouac one. Begrudgingly, my friend and I accepted her invitation to come to Chicago and house-sit her home over the summer while we looked for work. (Just in case I never told you, Sis, you significantly and positively changed my life with that one offer. Thank you.)

It was in Chicago that I decided to accept a position with the Platt Music Corporation, an electronics retailer who sold their merchandise through retail department stores transparently. What I mean by "transparently" is that if you went into a Marshall Field's store in Chicago and bought an appliance or stereo, you were actually buying it from Platt. So, in a way, I worked for Marshall Field's. It was later that I formally accepted a training position with Marshall Field's.

Anyway, with the new job came a new apartment, a nasty little thing that possessed the cockroaches I refer to in the preface to this book. A new era had dawned. An era that I will never forget.

I've tried.

I ate Underwood's Chicken Spread and Red Baron Pizza every day except Sunday and Monday.

I went to the Beacon Tap (I called it the Bacon Tip when I had stayed too long) every night and invented Ranch Doritos by dipping the nacho cheese versions in ranch dressing. Unfortunately, I never received proper recognition for this discovery. I would stay at the Beacon Tap until the bartender started to look attractive. That would take awhile.

I went to my sister's every Sunday and had dinner and brought home leftovers that I ate on Monday.

I did my job.

My new job was as a customer service representative (CSR). I was pretty excited. Here I was in Chicago, the windy city (actually the warehouse where I worked was in Des Plaines), working at Marshall Field's (actually Platt Music Corporation) and making $4.00--count'em, one, two, three, four dollars--EVERY hour (before taxes). It was heady stuff. Of course, they don't explain to you what a CSR does when they offer you the job. If they did, no one would take it.

I still remember walking in my first day. There was a feeling of foreboding, of eyes measuring me as I made my way to the two desks that faced each other in the middle of the open area of that warehouse office. It was almost like the people in the other departments were whispering, "Dead man walking." It wasn't until later that I discovered all the people in the delivery department, the parts department, the extended service plan department-- all of which formed a circle around customer service--had all spent time in customer service. They had either escaped or been paroled.

You see Marshall Field, the man, wrote a book called *Give the Lady What She Wants*. When I was there, the Marshall Field's customer service philosophy was extremely customer friendly. Sales associates were not allowed to tell a customer, "No." If a sales associate could not please a customer, he or she would involve a department manager. Managers did everything within reason, sometimes beyond reason, to keep the discerning customer of Marshall Field's happy. If the department manager also failed to pacify the customer, then the store manager would intervene with even more latitude to please the customer. If a customer's demands or demeanor was SO outlandish, SO incredibly unreasonable, SO nasty and uncivilized that none of these individuals could please them, then that person was referred to customer service.

Me.

Me and Jim Henson.

No, not the Muppets guy. Jim Henson was a five-year veteran of Marshall Field's electronics customer service department. He had watched others come and go, but he had stayed. His loyalty to the department had been rewarded with burnout--massive, extensive burnout--the type of burnout that can only be achieved by combining talent, compassion and drive with equal amounts of frustration. Jim Henson was talented. He was also tired. Jim was deep-fried to a crackly crunch.

For five years Jim had answered his phone knowing that the person on the other side of this impending conversation was irrational, angry, and near violence. For five years Jim had worked hard to reconcile these conflicts. Now, Jim was a crispy-critter. Jim was the kind of guy--cynical, gruff and belligerent in the way that people who know too much and have experienced too much can be--that other employees avoided.

Me, fresh off the turnip truck (or more accurately, the Greenup truck) and Jim Henson. Me, with the goofy smile of the eternally-clueless, and Jim with the perpetual scowl of the eternally-disgusted. We were quite the team.

And it worked. Initially I would listen in horror as I heard Jim manhandle a customer. At this level of interaction, the company didn't really care if we kept the person as a customer so long as the senior level executives didn't have to deal with them. Hence, Jim was free to resolve these issues as he saw fit, provided that the resolution was final. His side of the conversation might sound like this:

(phone rings)

"Henson," barks Jim as he breathlessly snatches the phone and does his best drill sergeant impression.

(listening)

"Is this going to be a long story, because I am very busy?" Jim grows impatient with the detailed story of past events that the customer feels compelled to share.

"Well, I don't like your attitude either, so we're on the same page there," Jim's eyes rolling involuntarily.

"Sure, I would be happy to transfer you to my manager. I'd be ecstatic just to get you off of my line."

And with that, Jim would extend the phone across his desk towards mine and state, "Mitchell, wanna be my manager?" It was more of a command than a request.

In that way my education on the fine art of service recovery began. Jim and I worked those phones madly. Occasionally, Jim would irritate a customer to such near psychotic levels of mental anguish that they would threaten to fling themselves into the window display of our downtown State Street store, and then he would transfer the call to me. That left me, all-mellow-farm-boy, to talk them off the ledge. I was all that, with a bag of chips and a dill pickle on the side. Until Ozzie. Ozzie Hasham. My personal anti-Christ.

OZZIE, JOHN CLEESE, AND BEHAVIORAL VIRUS INFECTIONS

You know how sometimes when you meet someone for the very first time you are immediately drawn to that person. The connection you experience with this complete stranger is immediate and strong. It is an amazing feeling to establish that instant rapport with someone. Then, of course, there is the opposite. Those occasions when you meet someone for the very first time and you feel a deep sense of repulsion. A feeling comes over you that indicates that if you never interacted with this person ever again, that would be okay. Ozzie Hasham fell distinctly into this latter category for me.

It started on a Monday. Ozzie had purchased some merchandise at our big warehouse sale over the weekend. The warehouse sale was our annual de-evolution into the retail equivalent of crack-cocaine dealing. Items were priced insanely cheap to unload them and shoppers descended on this event with the frothing mouth and darting eyes of a hardened addict three days past his last fix. Despite our best efforts to label every item "AS IS", the week following a warehouse sale was always mayhem in customer service. Customers calling wanting owner's manuals, turntable cartridges, connecting cables...and each armed with the assurances of a haggard sales associate who had told them these items were available by calling customer service. These were the same sales associates who had been procured from a temp agency two days before the event and told explicitly, "Whatever you do, don't promise a freaking turntable cartridge to these people." That was the entirety of their training.

Ozzie initially called about a remote control for his stereo system.

My recollection of the events that followed that first call are decidedly hazy. Much like the post-traumatic-stress-syndrome suffered by soldiers, I cannot remember distinctly what happened next. I do recall that the frequency of Ozzie's calls to me increased as the week progressed. It seems to me that the nature of his demands kept shifting as well. In my memory, Ozzie's original request broadened and shifted until, by Thursday, I could no longer tolerate any more interactions with Mr. Hasham. To me, the process of satisfying Ozzie Hasham bore an uncomfortable similarity to a snipe hunting trip I had experienced when I was eleven-years-old. Our final conversation was brief.

"Mr. Hasham," my voice raising and becoming higher in pitch, the latter quality an annoying by-product to my anger, "I don't think you know what you want. And until you figure out what is going to make you happy, I don't want you to call me ever again!" With that I slammed down the phone, hanging up in anger for the first time in my life.

Jim Henson leapt out of his chair in excitement. "THAT"S the way you talk to them! You're learning, boy. You've got potential. Now, you just need to do that on MONDAY, cause you're wasting time."

I remember feeling equal parts mad and embarrassed. "He deserved it," I said to myself, more to convince myself than anyone else. "Asshole."

After a few minutes I regained my composure and answered my phone again. "Marshall Field's Electronics Department, Customer Service. This is Dave. How may I help you?"

"May I speak to the manager please?"

Like I wouldn't recognize Ozzie Hasham's voice after a week's worth of phone conversations. "Of course. It would be my pleasure."

And then I looked across my desk at Jim Henson. "Jim, would you like to be MY manager?" I would show Ozzie, I thought to myself. He had the good cop. Now he's gonna get Jim Henson. He'll be begging for me. He didn't know how good he had it.

Jim's eyes widened as I made my offer. He had the look of a hungry lion moments before the raw meat is thrown into his cage. I even noticed a tiny bit of saliva trickling down the corner of his mouth. "Really?" Jim responded with a barely contained level of excitement that bordered on manic. "Put him through!"

I transferred the call to Jim and then sank back in my chair to await the pyrotechnics. My God, I thought to myself, this has the makings of a World Wrestling Federation Smackdown Main Event. Let's get ready to rrrrruuuuu ummmmmbbbbbllllle!

What happened next rivaled the UFO sighting I experienced in high school with my very good friend, Scott Shafer.

The Jim Henson I had worked with for the past year, the cantankerous burn-out who dispatched unhappy customers with the ease of a pest control professional, THAT Jim Henson disappeared. He was replaced by what George Bush #1 would have described as a kinder, gentler Jim.

"Good afternoon, Customer Service. This is Jim. How may I help you?" There was practically a lilt in his voice for Chrissake!

"Well, I am so sorry to hear that, Mr. Hasham. No, no, that is certainly not our policy. I don't know why this has been so difficult for you. Of course I wil. I will have that done for you today. Yes, I know Dave Mitchell. Well, Mr Hasham, not everyone is cut out for customer service."

As I listened to Jim's half of the conversation astonished and incredulous, it began to occur to me what was happening. Within 15 minutes, Jim had resolved a customer conflict that I had been working on for a week. Jim got a letter from Mr. Hasham, a letter that detailed for two paragraphs how fantastic Jim Henson was to work with. A letter he never showed to our boss, Shirley Guagenti, because it went into great detail in paragraph three about how horrible Dave Mitchell was. But Jim kept that letter in his top drawer and anytime I would start to get a bit full of myself, Jim would pull that letter out and say, "Remember Mr. Hasham, Dave? He didn't like you much, did he?"

As I watched Jim so effectively handle Ozzie Hasham, I realized that I must have contributed (perhaps created completely) this conflict. Now, there was no denying that Ozzie and I were two very different people. In Jungian psychological terms, it could be said that our interactive styles were exactly opposite. But that doesn't excuse my poor handling of the situation.

By the way, the concept of interactive styles is of keen interest to me. I am not going to delve into this complicated issue in this book, but I do enjoy speaking on this issue. In fact, I present Jungian psychological concepts on human interaction using different themes like Hollywood movie icons or wine-tasting events. These sessions are among my most popular seminars. I mention this because I love doing these seminars, make a large percentage of my income doing these seminars, and hope that you, as the reader of this book, may be in a position to hire me to do one of these seminars in the future. If this whole paragraph strikes you as gratuitous marketing and self-promotion, then you have interpreted its intent correctly. My children may well be sucking on washcloths for nourishment as you read this. Please hire me. Now, back to Live and Learn, or Die Stupid...

Besides the obvious difference between my style and Ozzie's, there were other reasons why my interaction with Mr. Hasham went awry. About a year later came the epiphany. This three-part epiphany was so simple, that I am almost ashamed to share it with you. It could damage my credibility-- provided, of course, that I have any credibility with you.

Moving forward about a year, I was now working as a store-trainer for Marshall Field's. It's funny now to look back on this period of my career. That job was my first real training position. I would provide training to the sales associates on how to run the cash register primarily, with some customer service skills thrown in--the same classes, the same content, day in and day out. I became so familiar with the content that I would often have out-of-body experiences while conducting classes. There I would be, hovering over the classroom, contemplating my weekend plans or grocery list, while simultaneously explaining how to process a credit-card purchase being sent out-of-state as a gift. In fact, during one class, not only did I drift away during my presentation, but I also tapped my purple flipchart marker incessantly against my hand. The result of this feverish tapping was a splatter pattern of fluorescent purple on the front of my crisp white shirt. At the lunch break, a thoughtful student pointed out the distracting behavior. I remember that day as being particularly influential in the development of my professional self-esteem. I shudder to think of the quality of those sessions.

Anyway, during the two-day cash register training class, there was a segment on customer service. The bulk of this segment was dedicated to a videotape. I no longer remember the title of the videotape, but I do know that the British comedic actor John Cleese starred in it and his company produced it. The tape was clever as you would expect from a Cleese influenced project, even one produced for the purpose of customer service education. The learning points were interwoven around a faux murder mystery. My three epiphanies mirrored the three major points about human behavior:

1. Behavior breeds behavior.
2. You choose your behavior.
3. Positive behavior overcomes negative behavior.

These concepts probably strike you as incredibly obvious. Nonetheless, I am going to explain them. It is what we speakers do, explain the obvious at length.

Behavior breeds behavior. I remember hearing about a study once, probably by Johns Hopkins since they seem to do almost all the noteworthy studies, on the source of stress for people while at work. The study concluded that the most prominent source of stress at work was interaction with other people. Duh. Big bag of duh! My dad, the appliance repairman, used to tell me this all the time when I was a youngster. He put it this way: "The world would be a wonderful place if it weren't for people."

Anyway, what "behavior breeds behavior" means is simply this: The way we treat someone has a huge bearing on the way that person will treat others. Put another way, if I am in a bad mood and treat someone else poorly, there is a good chance that this person will, in turn, now be in a bad mood and treat the next person accordingly. In this regard, my bad mood is like a viral infection. With each personal contact I have with another person, I spread my infected mood. I am the Typhoid Mary of behavior.

Conversely, the opposite is true. If I am in a good mood, my interactions with others impact them in a good way. In this scenario I am spreading joy. I like spreading joy and that gets us to the second point.

By the way, I notice that some people mistrust joy-spreaders. Have you noticed this? Often, when I am walking around with a smile on my face, making eye contact with others, and complimenting them, the response I get involves a furrowed eye brow, a quickening of someone's pace and short, and anxiety-filled replies. Maybe it's my technique.

You choose your behavior. Certainly the way you are treated by others can influence what behavior you choose, but ultimately the choice is still yours. I mean, have you ever been in a good mood? (If you answer this question with a "no," slowly put down this book, walk deliberately to the phone, calmly dial your local crisis center, and start your life anew.) Sure you have. How about the opposite? Have you ever been in a bad mood? Boy, howdy! So you know that your mood is not something you are born with. It is something you choose (unless you are suffering from depression or another mental health concern, and that is a far more complicated issue).

Barring health issues, our behavior is under our control. We make choices about our behavior based on internal and external influences, but the final decision is ours. Now, which state would you rather be in, a good mood or a bad mood? I'm thinking you'd rather be in a good mood. So why aren't we always in a good mood? Factors. External factors. Like other people. Sure, I completely understand. Having said that, reread the first chapter on *internal locus of control*. Be the hand and choose a good mood, because good moods are so much better than bad ones. That moves us to the third point.

Positive behavior overcomes negative behavior. Because healthy people would prefer to be in a good mood rather than a bad mood, positive behavior has an innate advantage over negative behavior. That means that if two people were interacting, one in a good mood and the other in a bad mood, eventually the one in a bad mood would convert to a good mood. Now, this doesn't always happen because you don't know how committed to the bad mood this other person is. However, one thing is for certain. If the good mood person gives up and lets the other person breed his behavior, therefore putting both of them in a bad mood, there is a whole new level of ugly behavior possible. Bottom line, even if your good mood doesn't convert the other person's bad mood, your good mood will at least help keep the bad mood from getting worse.

Now, back to Ozzie Hasham. Ozzie was in a bad mood. He had received what he considered to be poor service and had chosen a negative behavior as a result. That's not unusual. I initially tried to influence Ozzie's behavior with my positive behavior. Unfortunately the "behavior breeds behavior" phenomenon works both ways, and since Ozzie was more committed to his negative behavior than I was to my positive behavior, ultimately his behavior won. I became negative. Once I became negative, he went to a new, deeper level of negativity. I followed, and on it went into the abyss of conflict.

Enter Jim Henson. Because Jim wanted to cover my back, he was extremely committed to his positive behavior. Soon, Ozzie (who, like all healthy people, wanted desperately to be in a good mood) became influenced by Jim's good mood. The spiral that had gone down when Ozzie and I had interacted was now moving upward. Within a few minutes, Jim had resolved the issue.

Now, like I said, the different interactive styles that we all possess certainly have a huge impact on our interpersonal relationships. There are several great books about these issues. Heck, maybe I will write one if this one sells more than the handful of copies that I plan to buy personally. But no matter how well-versed we become on matters Jungian, I still believe that one of the best road maps for handling other people is the one that John Cleese taught me when I was about 23-years-old.

Behavior breeds behavior. You can choose your behavior. Positive behavior overcomes negative behavior.

Try it.

CHAPTER SEVEN

When Your Mojo Goes

SENSE OF HUMOR

Have you ever been a senior in high school? I have a theory about this crazy, complicated time. If you want to know what degree of cockiness you are capable of achieving, go back and examine your behavior during this time. I mean, come on, you've waited years for this. Freshman year, you are just a frightened little bunny trying to melt into the walls of high school. Though sophomore year feels a little bit better, the fact that there are still more kids older rather than younger than you can be intimidating. Junior year is like being the runner-up in a beauty contest: "Should the seniors be unable to fulfill their duties as seniors, the juniors will reign." Finally, senior year arrives. Boo-yah.

I had been honorable mention all-conference first baseman my junior year. Unmistakably, the entire purpose of baseball season my senior year was *my* pursuit of first team all-conference first baseman. Clearly, because the entire world was all about *me*. The only snag was we got a new baseball coach my senior year. Bob Gaddey. Apparently Coach Gaddey did not receive the advance publicity kit I had sent him in the mail. It was also apparent that Coach Gaddey was unaware that the entire world was all about *me*.

Coach Gaddey arrived at our school with a list of priorities for the baseball season. He gathered us together and shared some lunacy about teamwork and individual sacrifices for the greater good of the team. Whatever! Not one mention of *the* most important goal, *my* pursuit of first team all-conference first baseman.

This disparate opinion of the purpose of the baseball season came to an ugly apex during the fourth game of the season. We, the Cumberland Pirates, were playing the Martinsville Blue Streaks at Haughton Park in Greenup, Illinois. Both teams were 3 - 0, each having won two non-conference games and one conference game. This was an early battle for advantage in the hotly contested Little Illini Conference. You probably remember it? Spring 1979? It was in the Greenup Press, the weekly four-page newspaper. Sound familiar? Well, anyway, the story follows.

It's the bottom of the fifth inning. We're trailing 3 – 2. There is one out and a runner on first. I am coming to the plate. I bat third in the lineup. If you know anything about baseball, you know the third hitter has good power, good speed: probably your best natural athlete on the team.

Short pause here for the reader to realize that the preceding sentence should be perceived with the self-mocking sarcasm the writer intends.

As I step into the batter's box, I immediately begin my pre-at-bat ritual, all carefully designed to impress my girlfriend.

I dig in with my left foot (I am left-handed.) while keeping my right foot out of the batter's box, all the time surveying the positioning of all the fielders. It's a move that suggests I have such bat control that I can place a batted ball anywhere I want. I then bend down and pick up a handful of dirt, rubbing it onto my bat, onto my hands, and finally onto my pants. The first two are to improve my grip, the latter placement of dirt, onto my pants, is so if I fail to get on base during the game it will still appear as if I am an integral part of the action. (I was a very cerebral ballplayer.) Finally, I look down at Coach Gaddey at third base to give the appearance of getting a sign--a move I do as a formality because Coach Gaddey likes to feel involved in the game. It is my way of feigning respect.

With a runner on first and my power to the gaps, I can foresee scalding the first-belt high fastball into the right-center field grass and driving home the tying run. Heck, I might even jack that cheese-heater the Martinsville pitcher calls a "fastball" right over the right-field fence. Would you like honey, Mr. Pooh? Bring me a platter of your finest meats and cheeses! I can already imagine my picture on the front page of the Greenup Press.

My fantasy is harshly interrupted by the realization that Coach Gaddey has just rubbed his forearms (what we called "the sleeves"). This is the indicator sign. In baseball, there are signs that indicate there will be a sign. It is a very complicated sport.

Coach Gaddey follows "the sleeves" by touching his nose. Four letters in nose. Four letters in bunt. We aren't a bright bunch, so Coach Gaddey keeps the signs simple. He has given *me*, former honorable mention all-conference first baseman, senior, three-hole hitter, the BUNT sign. HELLO! I don't bunt. Freshmen bunt. Nine-hole hitters bunt. Not me. I don't even practice bunting. Shoot, I would have to look up bunt in the dictionary to spell it. I think bunt is a cake.

Well, dutifully, I square to bunt the first pitch. The pitcher fires a juicy, belt-high, fastball over the plate and I bunt it foul down the first base line. Now down 0 - 1 in the count, I know I am going to get some off-speed junk, probably a hook (that's baseball talk for a curveball) on the outside corner. "I ain't gonna hit his pitch," I say to myself, steeling my determination to lay off the junk and work the count back into my favor. As I complete my at-bat ritual, my eyes again meet Coach Gaddey's. Coach has now moved about a third of the way down the baseline and, more emphatically, signals for the bunt.

I respond with the "possessed pigeon" look. You know, that look pigeons get when they bob their head and bob their heads and then all of the sudden, out of the blue, cock their head back, set their gaze on something, and freeze. Weird. I always assumed it was some sort of demonic possession. Anyway, I am in utter disbelief. I shoot a glance to my comrades on the bench to see if they are witnessing this unfurling melodrama, but they are all experimenting with chewing tobacco and are too light headed to realize what is happening.

Again, I dutifully square to bunt. A lazy Uncle Charlie (That's more baseball talk for curve-ball--ain't baseball cool?) floats across the outside edge of the plate and I bunt it foul down the third base line. Now down 0-2 in the count I realize that I will have to give up my desire to drive a pitch into the gap. I can expect a steady diet of pitches that are high, low, outside or inside in an effort to entice me to swing at a bad pitch. My thought now is to battle off these pitches and try to work the count to full. I will try to take a pitch the other way, a single over the shortstop perhaps, and advance the runner, allowing my clean-up hitting teammate to experience the glory of driving in the tying and winning run. All of this is running through my mind. I don't even look for a sign from Coach Gaddey. I don't have to. He has now moved two thirds of the way down the third base line and is screaming at the top of his lungs, "BUNT THE GODDAMN BALL, MITCHELL!", in front of the entire student body of Cumberland High School.

Actually, there were only about 12 people there, most of them parents, but I like to remember the story as involving the entire student body.

In that moment, I make a decision--a decision that will change my life.

I don't bunt.

I don't even try to hit the ball.

I decide to draw the line right then. As the next pitch approaches the plate (low and inside) I flail at it, obviously intending on missing it. I then glare down the third base line at Coach Gaddey, drop the bat, whirl around on my heel like Baryshnikov, and return to the bench.

I remained on the bench for the next five games serving a suspension for insubordination.

Immediately after I decided on this strategy, I knew I had made a mistake. Still, being a typical 17-year-old boy, I was defiant. Later, when I returned home after the game, I subjected my father to what was probably a 30-minute harangue, a tirade about the injustice, the unfairness, the inequity, the evil incarnate that was Bob Gaddey.

To my dad's credit, he listened intently to my epistle. He didn't interrupt as I spewed bile for that half hour. When I was finished, Dad said, "Son, do you think you can change Bob Gaddey?"

I responded with that incredulous tone that only a teenager can truly manifest. "Noooo, I don't think I can change Bob Gaddey," came my sarcastic reply.

"Son, let me give you some advice that is gonna save you a bunch of heartache in your life."

Internally, my eyes were rolling and I sighed heavily. I say internally because I was quite afraid of my father and would not have risked inciting more anger in him by ACTUALLY rolling my eyes and sighing heavily. But I definitely did it internally.

"In life, if you can change it, change it...", he began. Funny, this sentiment is fundamentally the same thing as telling someone about the importance of an ***internal locus of control***. My dad was actually an amateur behavioral psychologist disguised as an appliance repairman.

"In life, if you can change it, change it: if you can't, laugh about it. You'll be a lot happier." Then my dad launched into his own epistle. It wasn't pretty. He told me that I was selfish. That my only concern was for my needs and not the needs of others.

On top of that, he added, I had made my life so important to me that it was funny to behold as an outsider. "Oh, you are funny, Son, but not in the way you want to be." He added, "If you don't learn to laugh at yourself soon, you are going to live a very miserable life."

Have you ever caught a bad-hop grounder right in the gazeechies? If you are a woman, you don't actually have gazeechies, but you get the picture. It hurts. Gazeechies, by the way, is a word my son Slade and I made up for testicles. Testicles is an ugly word to a kid. Gazeechies, on the other hand, is funny as hell. "Funny as hell" is an important balance for the pain of being hit in the gazeechies.

I thought about what my dad told me. Just like that, within a moment . . . like, you know, within ten years or so, I got it. (Just because your parents give you good advice doesn't mean you choose to apply it immediately. I remind myself of this every time I offer my thoughts to my teen-daughter, Brooke. I am sure she is storing my wisdom away, even though it appears that she dismisses my input as if it were the ramblings of a disturbed mind.)

You have to have a sense of humor to achieve contentment. I'm not talking about telling jokes either. I'm talking about recognizing the inanity of life. In particular, our own unique contribution to life's comedy. You have to be able to laugh at yourself. My dad had hit the nail on the head. My head.

On a side note, I don't know about your dad, but my father got much smarter as I got older. By the time I was 30, the man was a freaking genius. I don't know if he was taking ginkgo or some other brain-enhancing supplement, but he really sharpened right up. It's just a shame he wasn't brighter during my adolescent years. Dad passed away about a year before this book was sent to publishing. I sure miss him. The last chapter is dedicated to the wisdom he tried to impart in me in his own unique way.

WHERE DID THE MOJO GO

Many years later, after doing a keynote speech about these concepts, a gentleman approached me as the crowd dispersed. "I really enjoyed your presentation, but I have to disagree about the importance of a sense of humor. I am a serious man." The gentleman continued, "People appreciate my no-nonsense style. I don't kid around, and for that reason, I am highly respected."

I thought about what this man said for a little while and said, "I think you are wrong." Here's why.

Some days we--you, me, everyone--roll out of bed and we got the mojo working that day. We take a shower and do our hair and it looks perfect.

There's no traffic on the way to work. A parking place is just waiting for us. We resolve each issue effectively. We offer a wonderful idea at the staff meeting. We receive a commendation from a customer. Our boss pats us on the back. An attractive person smiles at us at lunch.

We are all that, a bag of chips, and a dill pickle on the side. We rock, we're hot, we're smokin', we got a shizzle in our nizzle (by the time this book is released, that will so not be current) cause, like I said, we got the mojo working. We go home after a day like that feeling like we've got it all figured out. Then we go to bed and get up the next morning...

And we got no mo' mojo. Where did the mojo go? We have been de-mojoed overnight.

We take a shower and spend 45 minutes doing our hair only to look like we have a hornet's nest on top of our head. We are 15 minutes late for work because of traffic. There isn't a parking space for miles. Every issue that was resolved yesterday has come undone. We sit in the staff meeting in what can only be described as a catatonic stupor. Ozzie Hasham is on hold on line one for us. There is a post-it note on our office door from our boss that says simply, "SEE ME." An attractive person backs into you knocking coffee down the front of your shirt and still doesn't acknowledge you.

Like I said, we got NO mojo. In the words of Mark Knopfler (*Dire Straits* leader), "Sometimes you are the windshield, and sometimes you are the bug." Well, today, my friend, you are the bug. For the last eleven years I have made my living doing speaking engagements. I get nervous every time. Why? Because I never know when the mojo is gonna leave me. Let me tell you, if you think losing your mojo is unpleasant, try doing it with 1,000 people watching you. Talk about a gut punch.

On the bug days, you need a sense of humor. Everyone has days like this. It's not always a day. Sometimes mojo just leaves for an hour. Could be during that very important meeting. You walk in, sit down, and soon you realize, "Damn, I didn't bring my mojo." Sometimes mojo leaves for a week, usually right before you go on vacation. Messes with you. You spend the whole vacation wondering if your mojo will ever come back.

I once had a mojo-free month. Horrible.

But now I have a theory about mojo. At this point we have to capitalize the word. I believe that Mojo sometimes feels like it is taken way too much for granted. You know, Mojo just isn't getting its props. So, to get your attention, Mojo leaves. I imagine Mojo saying to itself, "Yeah, let's see how well Dave does without me. He'll be begging for his Mojo in no time. No Mojo, no standing O!"

The more desperate you become, the more you then try to hide your lack of Mojo from others, and the longer Mojo stays away. It is a vicious, ugly cycle.

On the other hand, if you can laugh at yourself, that frightens Mojo. Mojo becomes worried that you might not miss it or that you think you can do without it. Then Mojo comes rushing back to you. Consequently, the best way to shorten Mojo-free periods is to laugh at your own mojolessness.

Well, that's my theory anyway.

All I know is that a lot of the negative behaviors that I have manifested: the fear, the mistrust, the untruths--were all related to trying to conceal insecurities and weaknesses. By admitting them, heck, by laughing about them, they suddenly shrink in importance. When the insecurities shrink, so does the fear, mistrust, and untruths. The space left behind by the shrinking of our insecurities is filled by the expansion of our contentment and happiness.

So laugh. But not at others. At yourself. Besides, you have so much more material to work with that way.

CHAPTER EIGHT

Wild Monkeys in Duncan, Oklahoma

THE POWER OF THE SMILE

So many times I have waited out flight delays, ate at Burger King, arrived at hotels at 2:00 A.M. (a few times at 6:00 A.M.!), walked around airport concourses for two, three, four hours or more, and I have found myself uttering, "The glamorous life of the speaker." Occasionally when working an event with my dear friend Jerry or my good buddy Barry, this glamorous life can be more bearable. But most of the time I am alone. Alone. It is the most alone that I ever feel. I hike for hours on end in the mountains, just me and the dogs (Martini and Rossi) and I never feel alone. In my mind there is no more lonely place than an airport full of people when a person is one thousand miles from home.

"The glamorous life of the speaker."

Of course there are the cities. Cities are cool--cool when you have someone to share them with. I love to go out on date night with my wife. I love to explore the hot spots with Jerry. San Francisco, fabulous city–great food and wine. Chicago–wonderful people. Houston–so many restaurants. New Orleans–so many memories, I just wish I could remember them all. Philadelphia--even more fabulous than I expected. Baltimore–also better than I expected. Austin–oh, that music scene. Miami–man, those folks are good-looking. Atlanta–a spectacular city. St. Louis–who knew? Los Angeles–so hip. Dallas–big hair. Portland (both Maine and Oregon)–as different as their geography. I started to list all the cities I've been to, but it is far too long of a list. For every city I've been to all over North American and Europe, there are memories. Most of the memories are good, but some are lousy. I've had to make it through some long, lonely, restless nights in many of these cities.

Then there's Duncan, Oklahoma.

I don't even remember why I was in Duncan. I was speaking somewhere—Halliburton, Brown and Root, I think. I remember landing at an airport and I'm pretty sure I was in Oklahoma City. I got into a van, a sort of modern day stagecoach really, and proceeded to bounce around with a full bladder for 90 minutes till we finally arrived at the kind of spot my wife's step-mom, Bonnie, would describe as "out where God lost his shoes." (I love these kinds of phrases. I remember my dad used to describe a particularly remote area as, "...out where the hoot owls date the chickens and the roosters don't care." Still makes me giggle.)

I remember a rather unassuming Holiday Inn in Duncan, Oklahoma, and a front desk clerk who called me by name when I walked in the door because I was the last person due to check in that night. I recall a television that had poor reception leaving me with only four clear channels of viewing.

I also remember the monkeys.

The wild monkeys of Duncan, Oklahoma.

I was watching the Discovery Channel. It was one of the four channels. C-Span, CNN, and PBS were the other three, I think. Anyway, the Discovery Channel had a special on primates. As I enjoyed my Pizza Hut pizza (or maybe it was Dominos, I'm not sure), I watched with riveted attention as the narrator discussed the non-verbal communication techniques of monkeys. Monkeys, apparently, are quite the non-verbal communicators.

As I'm watching this show, they illustrate how a monkey who passes through the territory of another monkey will show with a simple facial expression that he respects the resident monkey and intends no ill-will.

The monkey smiles--an exaggerated smile.

The narrator goes on to share with viewers that this exaggerated smile is also meant to show a measure of fear, in addition to respect, to the resident monkey. This, I learn, signals to the resident monkey that the trespasser plans no attack and is merely passing through.

All of this is communicated by the monkey's Joker-like smile.

Then the view shifts to a group of people riding a roller coaster. We watch as they ascend to the top of the ride. We then see the faces of each person as they crest that peak and begin the plummet downward to what must feel like certain death. Next the camera zooms in on how each one of them is displaying that same facial expression, like an involuntary display of respect and fear for the descent.

As I continued to watch I realized that I, too, had used this non-verbal communication technique. Back when my wife and I made our decision about the size of our family, we agreed on having two children, hopefully one boy and one girl. If necessary, we would reluctantly go up to three children to have representation of both genders, but that would be the max. As soon as we achieved one boy and one girl or three children, whichever came first, I would then see a doctor to experience a certain procedure to render me incapable of fathering any more kids.

Yes, the vasectomy.

As I write this, my son, whose arrival officially fulfilled our childbearing contract, just celebrated his twelfth birthday. I have yet to get a vasectomy. When my wife reminds me of our agreement, I flash the monkey's exaggerated smile--a show of respect and fear for my wife. I'm thinking that if John Bobbitt had seen the Discovery Channel that night and used this non-verbal communication technique, things might have gone a little better with Lorena.

The narrator continued his discussion of non-verbal communication by pointing out the effect of the human smile on interpersonal dynamics. His focus now was not on the exaggerated smile to show respect and fear, but rather the natural smile. He pointed out how this less exaggerated version is used daily to show alliance and friendship to others. It is a shortcut for accessibility. It is the silent way we spread joy.

That is when the pizza nearly fell off my lap.

So blinding was the epiphany that I nearly collapsed onto the floor.

I NEED TO SMILE MORE!

MATCHING THE OUTSIDE TO THE INSIDE

During my time in the corporate world, I often received feedback from others that I was somewhat intimidating. I never understood how I could have created such a reputation. I was from Greenup, Illinois! How in the world could I be intimidating?

After the monkey documentary, I understood why. I immediately ran into the bathroom at the Holiday Inn in Duncan, Oklahoma and started making faces at myself. I tried to recreate my most common facial expressions. I scared myself.

In that moment I realized I suffered from FBS...furrowed brow syndrome. I looked intense, even intimidating. Did you see *Toy Story II*? There is a scene in that movie where Mr. Potato Head puts on his "angry eyes." That was me. For the love of Benji, I thought. No wonder people think I am intimidating. Heck, I intimidate myself!

From that day on I made a commitment to smile more. It may well be the most important commitment to personal development I have ever made. No really, I mean it--just try smiling.

Human beings are susceptible to first impressions. We can't help it. We do judge books by covers. It's true we do rush to judgment. We install filters in our mind, positive or negative, based on those first pieces of information we receive about another person, place or thing. Once that filter is in place, we have a hard time changing our perception. Despite the fact that I was a happy, easy-going guy on the inside, I looked like an intense, serious, and intimidating person on the outside. My most common facial expressions were influencing how people responded to me.

Then, just like the monkey, I would react to people's reactions to me by being even more intense, serious, and intimidating.

My common facial expressions were changing the way I felt and acted. Oddly, I had always thought it worked the other way around. But the truth is, the way we look and the way we feel and the way we act are so intertwined that when we change one of these behaviors, any one of them, it also affects the other two.

Would you rather be happy, relaxed, content, and joyous or would you prefer to be intense, restricted, stressed, and intimidating? I wanted to be the former. To do so, I decided I would spend more time looking like I felt that way.

I started smiling.

And smiling.

I practiced smiling at airports. Nobody smiles at airports. It was an amazing experience. I started to meet more pleasant people. I received better customer service. More people started conversations with me. I got upgraded more often. Bartenders bought me drinks.

I smiled at the gym. People started to remember my name. I started feeling sort of popular. People would remark that I was always in a good mood.

Nothing significant had changed in my life except that I was now making it a point to smile more often. Because of that one change of behavior, my reputation changed 180 degrees. You know what else? I felt happier. As a result of the way people were treating me, I WAS in a good mood more often--all because of a smile.

That is how powerful a smile can be.

It's hard to estimate how many people are truly happy in this world. I can confidently say, however, that there sure are a lot of people who aren't happy. I used to fantasize about being that magical genie who could grant three wishes for all of humankind. The three things I would wish for are that all people would have high self-esteem, that all people would have an ability to be resilient under stress, and that all people would smile. The first two would probably require a genie's intervention, but smiling could be accomplished immediately.

It is the simplest damn thing, but I am telling you, smiling works. I probably should have started with this suggestion, but I might have reduced my credibility even further by starting with such a fundamental notion. I figure if you have read until this point, you either have WAY too much free time, or you like what you are reading.

Either way, I encourage you to slap on a grin and notice what impact it will have on your life experience.

Just try it.

Smile.

CHAPTER NINE

Song for My Father

I am about done.

The experience of writing a book on what I have always talked about has been amazingly interesting. There's more I could say, but I'm getting tired of my own voice, so you might be, too. Plus, I need to save some stories for the sequel!

We've talked about several concepts that have helped me in my pursuit of happiness and contentment. These were:

- ➤ Internal Locus of Control
- ➤ Individual Interpreted Reality
- ➤ Positive Self Talk
- ➤ Positive Focus
- ➤ Promoting Seamwork
- ➤ Understanding Human Behavior
- ➤ Maintaining a Sense of Humor
- ➤ The Power of the Smile

These are all great concepts, at least for me. I hope something may have struck you as valuable. But to wrap up this book, I want to pay special tribute to my father.

Dad died in January 2005. He was 83-years-old. Most of his life, and the entirety of my life, he lived in Greenup, Illinois. He owned Mitchell's Heating and Air Conditioning. He coached Little League Baseball. He supported many organizations both publicly and privately. He was active in the Presbyterian Church until becoming disillusioned with the politics of it all. He fought in World War II. He married when he was 20-years-old and stayed with the same woman, despite her many troubles, until she died over 50 years later.

Most important to me, however, is this man raised me.

I found out about my father's death while speaking to a group of claims adjusters at Allstate Insurance in Roanoke, Virginia. (By the way, some of the most gracious people I have ever met were in the Roanoke office that day, including the manager, Herb Roper. I will never forget the kindness extended to me by everyone there). I left Roanoke, flew to Chicago, and drove to the funeral with my sister. The day we buried our father was brutally cold.

And no one showed up.

Oh, there were the Masons to deliver final rites and some veterans for the military salute. A couple of people who were not required to attend did show up (thank you Tim Yaw and Tim Jackson). But for a lifetime of 83 years, few people attended.

Wow, I thought, so this is what it comes down to. One's entire life can be culminated with a few words and even fewer in attendance. My grief was punctuated by the firing of the rifles and the lonely sound of "Taps" as the funeral concluded. (Man, whoever wrote "Taps" nailed it. That is one sad tune.)

The whole affair did not seem commensurate with the impact this man had on my life. Therefore, I decided to extend the tribute to my dad in my own way. Since I get to appear in front of approximately 10,000 people each year, I make it a point to include some piece of my father's wisdom in every speech I make, somehow. I also decided that whenever possible I would request "Song for My Father" by Horace Silver. (Sullivan's Steakhouse in Houston is a particularly good place to accomplish this, I found. Hey, if I'm going to honor my father, might as well throw in a well-prepared filet mignon and a nice glass of wine.)

Since I am winding down this book, let me throw out one more tribute to my father. We'll call these the "Dale-isms". Like I mentioned earlier in the book, Dad had a saying for every situation--many clichés, a few originals. Now that I am a father, I find all of these pearls of wisdom coming out of my lips directed towards my own kids. So, here's to you, Dad. I hope you are happy and content wherever you may be.

> "I love you boy, but damn..."
> "No good deed goes unpunished..."
> "Some cook, some clean and some just eat..."
> "Cheer up. It's gonna get worse..."
> "Don't try to teach a pig to dance. You'll get frustrated and the pig will get mad..."
> "I was so poor growing up that I ate nothing but jam sandwiches...You know what jam sandwiches are? Two pieces of bread jammed together."
> "Do something...even if it's wrong."
> "That guy talks like a man with a paper ass."

"He lives out where the hoot owls date the chickens and the rooster don't care."

"Act like you know what you're doing. By the time they realize you don't, you'll be gone."

"If you can change, change it. If you can't, laugh about it."

"In a hundred years, it won't matter."

"Did anyone die? Then how bad can it be."

and. . ."Son, if it makes you happy, that's all that matters."

This last one didn't pass his lips until he was quite old, and always with a soulful, prolonged, and deeply melancholy gaze. Dad, you did good, and I love you.

There have been many other extremely important people in my life. My wife Lori has been absolutely the most important person to me for over 20 years and will always hold the most special place in my heart. My children, Brooke and Slade, are amazing--sources of such pride and joy that exceed anything I could imagine. I am so lucky to have a sister that is as intelligent and caring as Diana. My dear friends, Jerry, Dennis, and Scott, are incredible people who have provided me with many shared special memories.

I have been fortunate to have worked for and with so many talented professionals: Ted Steele, Bob Atkinson, Susan Wally, Jim Henson, Max Suzenaar, Bob Stolz, Susan Meeske, to name just a few. In addition, I have had, and still have, the pleasure of working with some brilliant people as clients. The list is endless and no effort to capture all the names of those who have influenced me could be complete.

Perhaps, ultimately, that is the most important element of contentedness—the relationships that develop over time. I think it is this connectedness to each other that insulates us from the rigors of life's challenges.

As I said in the preface to this book, I am just an average guy. But I have amazing loved ones, and I am so much better as a result. So while I continue to live and learn, at the very least, I know one thing for sure: when I look around at the company I keep, I will <u>NOT</u> die stupid!

Printed in the United States
90676LV00003B/1-108/A

OTHER BOOKS BY DOROTHY FULDHEIM

A Thousand Friends
I Laughed, I Loved, I Cried

THREE
AND A HALF
HUSBANDS

Dorothy Fuldheim

SIMON AND SCHUSTER · NEW YORK

Published by Simon and Schuster
A Gulf+Western Company
Rockefeller Center, 630 Fifth Avenue
New York, New York 10020
Designed by Edith Fowler
Manufactured in the United States of America
1   2   3   4   5   6   7   8   9   10

Library of Congress Cataloging in Publication Data

Fuldheim, Dorothy.
    Three and a half husbands.
    I.   Title.
PZ4.F964Th   [PS3556.U33]   813'.5'4   76–15221
ISBN 0–671–22321–6

I would like to thank Ladislas Farago for his help in researching information on the American forces in France in 1917.

For my daughter, Dorothy

1

What is a smile worth? No one can calculate its value. My Aunt Molly had a smile that enchanted everyone. It lit up not only her face but the room where she was sitting. The gods had been good to Aunt Molly, because she had a wealth of auburn hair with a touch of gold and a wide mouth with very white teeth and that wonderful smile. Her skin was white and her figure like an hourglass, and she used that figure effectively whenever a male was near, moving as sinuously as a cat. Her theory was that males respond with ardor to a female if she reveals that she is a womanly woman, and my Aunt Molly was the epitome of femaleness in all its dimensions: sex lure, tenderness, willfulness, courage and originality. Her eyes were made to flutter with a come-on look; her hands white and soft, to be held; her throat, to be kissed; and her lips to promise sweetness.

She was my favorite relative and fascinated me with her ideas. For example, she once worked in a blouse factory, but she hated going to work. She explained that this was because she had to get up early in the morning, which did not agree with her.

"For me to get up in the morning," she insisted, "is not good." Her theory was that the morning sun was best for sleep. "That's when your strength and health are fortified," she told me.

"Where did you get that idea?" I asked her. I had never heard that any scientist had done research on such a possibility.

My Aunt Molly looked at me with patience. "I should wait for a scientist to tell me what I know! I know what I know." And having decided that her theory was fact, Aunt Molly operated as though it were a law of nature.

Aunt Molly also decided that the only way she could sleep late in the morning was to quit her job and get married. Finding a husband was no problem.

She had merely to smile her ravishing smile, undulate her sinuous body, heave her magnificent breasts, and the male she had set after had no chance—caught by her loveliness and coquetry.

The most available male for Molly at the time was the superintendent of the blouse factory. He had as much chance of escaping as the fly in the spider's web. That Bill was a widower with three young sons didn't worry Aunt Molly. My mother, Molly's sister, was the one who did the worrying.

"Molly, three boys," she warned, "are not easy to take care of. That's worse than a job! What do you know about boys?"

"So, what do I have to know about boys?" argued Molly. "They should wash their faces, go to school, do their homework. Do I have to take a course about boys? Foolishness, Bertha!"

So Aunt Molly wore a diamond and a wedding band and could sleep as late as she liked; and Bill, the superintendent of the blouse factory, once again had a wife, and his three boys had a mother; and we had all the blouses we could wear, because Aunt Molly's philosophy was that an aunt should not go visiting empty-handed. From that time on we had blouses coming out of our ears—at least a three-year supply. And Aunt Molly grew more beautiful, as if to prove her point that the morning sun was good for one's health.

For three months Molly had her morning hours of sleep. Bill, the superintendent, was bewildered by Molly, her loveliness and her ideas; and the three boys were awed. But then, suddenly, it was all over, for Bill mistook the elevator door at the factory for an office door and fell down the elevator shaft. Molly was left a widow, the blouses ended, the three boys were once again orphaned, and Aunt Molly gave up her sunlit morning sleep and went back to her old job.

But she still had her swaying figure and her smile, the beautiful hair curled around her white throat, and her laugh, the laugh of a radiant woman. Men still pursued her. This time it was the custodian of the building who fell for her.

"I know," she said, "I should wait a year, but it's too much to take care of the three boys alone."

My mother was aghast. "Three months ago Bill died, and already she is talking of marriage. What kind of a sister have I got? What will all the neighbors say?"

"I think they should say," I told my mother, "that my Aunt Molly is wonderful. Who else would take three orphaned boys? She could send them to an orphan asylum, but Aunt Molly said, 'I should die first. Such nice boys, and they look at me with such frightened eyes.

" 'What will you do with us, Aunt Molly?' they ask.

" 'What will I do with you? They should live so long who say that I should give you up. You will stay with me.' "

So Aunt Molly got another diamond ring and married Al, the custodian of the factory. And though there were no more blouses, the custodian had a carriage, and when he and Molly came to visit, we knew that we now had a rich aunt and that Molly had gone back to sleeping late in the morning.

A few months after Molly married Al, his sister died and left a son, Douglas, twelve years old. Aunt Molly brought the orphan home and informed Bill's three sons that they would all have to help take care of him. I thought my mother would have a nervous breakdown.

"Molly, four boys! You are out of your mind!"

"What difference does it make? One more or less is of no consequence."

But alas, Al was repairing something on top of the building and fell off the roof and broke his neck, leaving Aunt Molly widowed once more—now with four children.

A settlement was made by the owners of the building, from which Molly received $3,500. This time Aunt Molly was really rich, so she bought herself a house and a beautiful black outfit. A friend learned about Molly and came to see her. "I've got the man for you. He is a widow with five children, all boys."

Aunt Molly turned white. "Five more boys!" she exclaimed.

"So what?" said her friend. "Five—seven—eleven. What difference does it make? He's got a good job. He is a superintendent in a beer plant."

"No," protested Aunt Molly. "I had one superintendent, I should take another one? And please, don't bother me with your proposal."

"All right, all right, who's forcing you? But would it hurt to look at him? Looking doesn't cost any money, and if you like him, you can look again. If you don't, you can send me a bill for forcing you to meet him. So, is that a good arrangement?"

After all, Aunt Molly did have the new outfit. And she had not been married to either of her two husbands long enough to feel any real grief, so she let herself be persuaded to meet the beer superintendent.

Aunt Molly married again, and now there were nine boys in her household, all noisy and boisterous and healthy, and all learning to love Aunt Molly.

Aunt Molly's marriage to Sol, her third husband, lasted less than two years, for Sol contracted pneumonia and died within two weeks. Aunt Molly, normally vivacious and cheerful, began to believe that hers was a strange fate.

She was distraught. "Why would God do this to me? Who else in the whole world's buried three husbands in five years? What does God mean by this?"

The nine boys surrounded her. "Aunt Molly, don't cry," they pleaded, but as she wept, they all began to weep, too. What could anyone say?

"How does it happen," Molly asked my mother, "that other women marry and stay married for forty and fifty years but I lose my husbands right away?"

In the midst of her tears she noticed her hat. It was brown. She needed a black hat. No one in the family had one.

"But why, Aunt Molly? What difference does it make whether you wear a black hat or a brown one? What earthly difference can it possibly make?" I asked.

"Do you hear that, Bertha, what your daughter is saying? What difference will it make? I should go to the funeral of my third husband and wear a brown hat? If it were my first husband or even my second, but for the third? How would it look if I wore a brown hat, I ask you," she demanded.

There was no use in arguing with Aunt Molly. A black hat she would have to have.

Kenneth, one of Molly's first husband's sons, said, "All right, Aunt Molly, you will have a black hat," and he proceeded to haul out his liquid black shoe polish. He covered Aunt Molly's brown straw with the black polish and then presented it to her.

"What about these?" asked Aunt Molly, indicating the white flowers on the hat.

"Give it back," said Kenneth, and he proceeded to paint the flowers black.

"Now," I said to Molly, "you've ruined the hat. Where else can you wear it?"

"With Molly's luck her fourth husband will die, and she will have a hat ready," my mother said.

At this, Aunt Molly rose from her chair and addressed all of us. "You should all listen to me and hear what your Aunt Molly has to say. You, Kenneth, who are the eldest, and Robert and Douglas. And you, my sister; and you, my brother, Sam. And you, my niece" —turning to me. "On this day I call on God to listen to me. I know what God wants. Maybe He doesn't speak to me like He did to Moses, but this is not the ancient times. But He spoke to me. 'Molly,' He said, 'you are not ever to get married again, because whoever you marry will die.' I am telling all of you—my sons, my niece, my sister and brother—no more marriages for me."

We were silenced. It was true that Sol was Molly's third husband and that each one of them had died before the end of the second year of their marriage. To hold God responsible for their deaths, that we could understand; but to say that God had doomed Molly and that for some inscrutable reason known only to the Deity any man she married was doomed to die soon afterward—this left us all in consternation.

My mother said, "Another Moses. And when did you speak to God that you know all this?"

By this time Molly was wringing her handkerchief. "To you He would have to speak. But to me, He doesn't have to use words. Am I such a fool that I don't understand Him? Tell me, if you are so smart, who else do you know who has buried three husbands? Mrs. Ginsburg's husband lost a foot. They had to cut it off. Did he die? No, he wears a false foot. Mrs. Epstein's husband had pneumonia. Did he die? The doctors gave him up, but what does Mr. Epstein do? He gets better! But me, Molly, has buried three husbands in five years. When my Sol got sick, the doctor said, 'Don't worry, he'll be all right. But my Sol isn't Mr. Epstein. As soon as the doctor left, what does my Sol do—he opens his eyes and says, 'Coffee, Molly,' and dies. Whoever heard of a husband asking for coffee and then dying? Who else do you know? Whoever heard of such a thing that a man with two eyes that can see should fall down an elevator shaft? Why in all the United States of America does my Bill have to step into an elevator that isn't there? You tell me why?"

"But, Molly," remonstrated her brother-in-law, "other husbands die. You are not the only one who loses a husband."

Molly turned on him. "Sure, sure, I know other

15

husbands die, but if you are so smart, tell me one other woman who you know who has lost three husbands."

We were again silenced.

"You see, there is a curse on me. I'll wear this hat this time, to the funeral, and I'll never wear it again, because I'll never marry again."

"You shouldn't talk so silly," said Sam. "You are not God."

"So, I'm not God, but I won't get married, and I'll take care of the nine boys, and I'll be a father and mother to them."

Her family protested, "Molly, nine boys—you'll go crazy."

"So," said Molly, "what should I do with them? Throw them out on the street? I'm a rich woman now. Bill left me $5,000 in his will; Al, 3,500; and Sol, 8,000. On $16,500 the boys and I will live."

Kenneth, the oldest, was thirteen, and the youngest, Michael, was three. In the early 1900s, $16,500 was a lot of money, but the family warned her that she would have trouble with the boys.

"Me?" said Molly, "I've had trouble—three husbands—God has done enough to me. I've agreed no matter what—no more husbands. So, God should please let me alone." She always talked about God as though He were a relative and they had a direct line of communication.

Aunt Molly was sad and silent. Her violet-blue eyes, with their long lashes, were often filled with tears. With nine boys it was imperative that she get a job. Nothing could persuade her to give up the boys. "No," she said, "they are mine and God wants me to keep them." There was no use in arguing with Molly about God.

"Aunt Molly," I suggested, "you will get married again."

"So, tell me who would marry me with nine children?"

"Molly, they are not your responsibility. Their relatives should care for them."

"Responsibility, schmonsibility!" was Molly's retort. "Of course they are mine. Sol wouldn't rest in his grave if he thought they were not with me." And then she repeated, "I'm not ever going to get married again, because if I do, the man will die."

"Nonsense," my mother responded, "why should he die?"

"Well," asked Aunt Molly, "if you are so smart, why did three of them die? They were alive until they married me."

My mother gave up arguing with her. But when Aunt Molly said she wouldn't marry anyone, she didn't mean she would be without a man. That was a life too bleak for her. She met other custodians and other superintendents; she wouldn't marry them. They could be her lovers, but no marriage. She had developed a real phobia about marriage, and nothing could sway her.

At one time, the man of the moment was the owner of a butcher shop. She explained that, in her position, it was good to be friendly with the owner of a food store because there were nine boys to feed.

After a year, her butcher friend contracted pneumonia but recovered, and Molly triumphantly pointed out that this was proof that she was right. He didn't die—he survived. If she had been married to him, she knew, he would have died. Who could argue with such logic?

After the butcher recovered, she lost interest in him. It was as though she had proved her point and had no further use for him, or perhaps it was because there was someone new on the horizon. This time it was an osteopath. We didn't know what an osteopath was, so we looked up the word in the dictionary—and Aunt Molly took on added stature. But the osteopath didn't last long; the boys didn't like him, and that really influenced Aunt Molly.

Aunt Molly had ideas of her own about how to bring up the boys and how the insurance money should be spent.

The oldest of the nine boys, Kenneth, was thirteen. Molly lined them all up, from the five-year-old to the thirteen-year-old, and made a speech.

"I am now," she said, "both your father and your mother. The insurance money will be put away for the three oldest boys' college education; then those three will work and provide the money for the younger ones' educations. We will all," she said, "sign such an agreement."

I still have that agreement among my cherished possessions. The agreement reads, "I, Molly Davidson, promise to raise Kenneth, Michael, Robert, Douglas, Donald, Victor, Jonas, Isadore, and Irwin. From this day, June 12, 1903, they will be my true sons and they will educate each other. When the first one is finished with college, he will help the next one. I want for each to be a doctor or a writer or a lawyer or an engineer, but no superintendents. So help me, God. Signed, Molly Davidson."

Her signature was followed by that of all the boys except Michael, who drew a circle, since he was too young to write.

Bill had bought a large house, with six bedrooms, so Molly easily made room for all the boys. She had some of them double up and allocated the largest room to the three youngest. The attic was a storeroom for their possessions, and the basement accommodated some of their activities—practicing on the trombone and their violins and Jonas' wood carving. In the dining room, there was a table big enough for fourteen. Molly always had the meals in the dining room; the kitchen wasn't big enough for all nine and herself. Washing the linens each week, and the boys' shirts and socks, was a job, but Mrs. Kolensky, a widow, was hired to do the housework.

The house rang with singing and laughter. Sometimes Molly thought how nice it would be to have a quiet house, but mostly she adjusted to the boys' boisterous hours, for she felt peace within herself. It was her atonement to the three husbands who had died so prematurely, as if it were her fault. Somehow she felt she had not loved them enough. At least she would care for their sons.

The bathroom was the real problem, but Molly was equal to all problems. A schedule was made out allocating five minutes each morning for washing and brushing teeth, and the time for each of the boys was pasted up in the bathroom. Bathing, also, was listed—two for Monday night, two for Tuesday, and so on. The basin and the tub had to be left spotless for the next in line.

Molly dreamed of having a second bathroom. A bathroom for herself with a place for her perfume, her cosmetics and her trinkets. Molly was sybaritical. She loved beautiful things around her. She rejoiced in dresses that swished as she moved. Frequently she used one kind of perfume on her skirt and another kind on her blouse. Her three husbands had had good incomes and had indulged her tastes. They could afford it.

Because she had worked in the blouse factory before her marriage, and earned only a small wage, the luxury her husbands had planned for her was intoxicating. She reveled in her new opulence. And conscious of what she owed them, she transferred to their sons her sense of obligation to the three husbands.

The boys knew that Molly wanted a second bathroom, so they saved their money, and by Christmas they were the proud owners of $37.19. They presented the money with great solemnity to Molly and told her that now she could have her second bathroom.

So Molly had a new bathroom installed, which was known as the Christmas bathroom. Further, the boys told Aunt Molly that it was to be her own exclusive bathroom. Molly cried.

"Aunt Molly, aren't you pleased?"

"Of course, but you should know my heart hurts when I am happy."

"Oh well," explained Irwin, one of the twins and thus the second eldest, "maybe Aunt Molly's heart is different than other people's."

Aunt Molly did take care of the boys, and it was something to see all of them sitting at the table. She never brought them all to our house at one time, because there wouldn't have been enough room. How those boys worked! They peddled papers; they ran errands for the neighbors; they worked at the butcher shop; they helped the janitor at school. And they pooled their money. There was only one bicycle, and each boy had an assigned day to use it.

On report card day, Aunt Molly would sit and solemnly scrutinize each card before signing her name. The devotion of all the boys to one another was remarkable. No fights at school without the whole gang defending one another. They were known as The Davidson Gang and had no trouble. No one attacked any one of them, because if anyone did, the whole group would turn on him.

Molly had a unique method of bringing up the boys. Douglas, Molly's son by courtesy of Al, her Episcopalian husband, was a quiet boy of twelve given to reading everything he could lay his hands on. Molly would sometimes say to him, "Douglas, come back from wherever you are; you have to live in this world. What's the matter, honey boy? Don't you like this world? Stop reading so many books. I don't want you to be like the Goldberg boy. He reads so much he has to wear double glasses."

If she had a favorite, it was Douglas; for he was a reflective child, but he was not shy. When there was something that he was interested in or wanted, he would sturdily defend his position. While he was still twelve he informed Aunt Molly that he was not going to go to Sunday school any longer.

"Why?" asked Molly. "All nice boys go to Sunday school. What will the neighbors think if you don't go?"

"I won't go," said Douglas, "because I don't believe in God."

This stumped Molly. "How can a little boy like you say he doesn't believe in God?" she asked.

"What has my size got to do with it?" retorted Douglas. "My brain is just as big as Kenneth's, and he's thirteen."

"You see," said Aunt Molly triumphantly, "that's

what becomes of all of this book business. Your nose is always stuck in some book."

"Well," asserted Douglas, "I don't believe in Him, so I'm not going. Besides, our Sunday school teacher is a dope and her nose is always red."

"So," said Molly, "we'll get you a teacher with a white nose."

"I'm not going," Douglas persisted.

"Listen to the little punk," said Kenneth. "Who do you think you are saying you're not going to Sunday school?"

"Just your little brother," said Douglas. "And what's more, you can talk—you don't have to go."

"Well, I did, didn't I; and wasn't I confirmed?"

But Molly was a pragmatist. She knew that the neighbors would talk if one of the boys didn't go to Sunday school. They would hold her sinful ways responsible. So she tried another tack with Douglas. "All right, you don't believe in God. Do you have to tell the whole world? Did they ask you if you believed in Moses and the Disciples and all the other Biblical figures? No one asked you. So, why can't you go as a favor to me? I'll give you a dime every Sunday for going."

The dime was too much for Douglas. It was a munificent sum to receive every week, so he yielded. "All right, just so you understand I don't believe in all that dribble," warned Douglas.

This was too much for the other boys. "Why should he get a dime for going to Sunday school?" They didn't.

Molly said, "Well, it's easier for you, because Douglas is an Episcopalian, and his religion is harder to understand and believe than yours."

2

One Monday evening, Aunt Molly and Douglas came to visit us. My mother put the tea kettle up and brought out a jar of peach jam. We all sat around the kitchen table.

"Tea," said Aunt Molly, "is good for only one thing, and that is as a conveyor of jam, and it has to be peach jam."

"Why," I asked, "does it have to be peach jam? Why not strawberry?"

"Because," said Aunt Molly, "you should know that the sun kisses peaches and gives them a pink glow."

"So," I said, "it gives them a pink glow. So what?"

Molly mimicked me, "So what. So it goes to the skin and makes the cheeks pink."

"How does the jam know to go to your cheeks and not to your buttocks?"

"First of all," answered Aunt Molly, "you should not talk with such words as 'buttocks.' It's not nice in front of your relatives, and why should it go to where you said? You should know why it doesn't go there. The jam is refined and wouldn't want to go to anywhere but the cheeks."

Douglas was listening, fascinated by Aunt Molly's curious logic, which defied all known laws of physiology, gravity and chemistry. She interpreted the world and the order of the universe according to what seemed to her reasonable and sensible standards, and that this confused and bewildered others only convinced Aunt Molly that she was logical in a world of irrationality.

"Aunt Molly, what's the matter with 'buttocks'? It's a perfectly good word and everyone has one. What would they sit on if they didn't?"

"So, if you use it to sit on, why should the sun waste its color on it?"

Douglas gave up. Aunt Molly's reasoning was too much for him.

"Do me a favor, Douglas," she said. "Go home and do your homework or whatever you want to do and let me talk to my sister."

Douglas reached for his cap.

"You are going without kissing Aunt Molly good night?"

Aunt Molly insisted on the ritual of kissing whenever the boys left her. It should, she explained, show them that they belonged to her. They should not feel alone in the world. After all, she was both father and mother to them.

When Douglas left, my mother asked, "So, what's your problem?"

"Well," said Aunt Molly as she stirred her jam, "I've met a man."

My mother said, "So when haven't you met a man? Every day you meet a man. Three husbands and already you've had how many suitors since? People will talk, Molly. A widow should be careful."

"For whom should I be careful?" said Aunt Molly. "I like to dance and to laugh, and my three husbands —may they rest in peace—did me no good."

"All right, all right. I don't say you should stay home and cry. You should live the kind of poor life we live. I don't want that for you. But, Molly, with three husbands!"

"Dead husbands," said Aunt Molly. "What good are they?"

"But, Molly, the nine boys. Why do you keep them? Send them back to their families."

"I should send them back," protested Molly. "What kind of monster do you think I am? They are mine and my responsibility."

"Then," my mother said, "you will have to stop going out dancing with Phil Lewis or whatever is his name." Now my mother was wrought up and she couldn't be stopped. "How does it look, tell me, for you, a widow three times with nine children, going out with a younger man to dance? I tell you, Molly, it doesn't look good. What will the Rabbi say? People will talk."

Molly pushed her tea away. "So, my three husbands died. Did the sun stop shining? Did the flowers stop growing? Do the stars refuse to come out at night? Have the birds stopped singing? Why should I stop living? Why shouldn't I dance and be happy? God didn't tell me to stop living. He must want me to be happy, but for some peculiar reason He doesn't want me to get married."

"What do you know about God's intentions?" my mother said.

"I don't," answered Molly, "but you must admit He does some strange things.

"Like what?" I put in.

"Well," answered Aunt Molly after a few moments' reflection, "look what he did to Abraham Lincoln?"

This nonplused me. What about Abraham Lincoln? I thought she was referring to his assassination, but not Aunt Molly. Her reflections were not historic but purely personal.

"He had trouble with his wife," Molly went on. "She spent too much money. Why should God allow such a wonderful man to have a wife that caused him trouble? And look what he did to the Jews. He gave us a Messiah and then took him away and gave him to the Gentiles."

This was too much for my mother. "Molly, for God's sake, what has all this got to do with you going out with so many different men?"

"Well," said Aunt Molly, "should I say to God, 'It's very nice of you to send me so many men for me to go out with and have a good time, but I can't do it because people will talk.' Listen, Bertha, if God sends them to me, He will take care of the gossip. Besides, Phil Lewis makes a good living. He sells musical instruments, and Kenneth wants to be a violinist."

"So," exclaimed my exasperated mother, "so Kenneth wants a violin. I want a carpet for my bedroom. So what has that got to do with your dancing with that Lewis?"

Molly took another teaspoon of jam. Why drink tea when there was jam?—there was nothing the matter with her figure. "After a few more dates with Lewis, Kenneth will get a violin."

I interrupted Aunt Molly. "Could you do us a favor and go out with a carpet salesman? Then your sister wouldn't have to mop her bedroom floor. You could get a carpet for her."

My mother said, "Stop talking such foolishness."

"Aunt Molly," I asked, "am I talking foolishness? If Kenneth can get a violin, why not a carpet?"

Aunt Molly said, "Lewis is a nice man, and maybe he will introduce me to a carpet man. For my sister I would like a blue carpet—it goes with her eyes."

My mother lapsed into her favorite Jewish phrase: "*Verdrei mir nicht mein kop* ["Don't mix up my head]," she said. "We're not talking about my carpet; we are talking about Lewis."

"All right," said Aunt Molly, "but when Kenneth gets his violin, and Robert his drum—he already has seven dollars saved—maybe I'll stop going out with Mr. Lewis."

3

Rabbi Kantrovitz, who had been with the Temple for ten years, was a man in his early forties. He had a warm smile and was friendly and outgoing, but he was inclined to give interminable sermons. He was liked and respected by the congregation, but they avoided his Friday night sermons.

He had heard about Aunt Molly and the nine boys, and eventually he decided to visit them. He had also heard she was beautiful. Mostly he was intrigued and curious to meet a young woman who had adopted nine boys. He wanted to discover what she was like and whether she was really devoted to the boys. Also, he was told that not all the boys were Jewish. One was an Episcopalian, and the others, he had heard, were Baptists. For some reason he had been reluctant to call on Aunt Molly. What could he say to console a woman three times widowed with nine boys and of different faiths? In all his rabbinical career he had never encountered such a situation.

It was after these thoughts that he resolved to face Aunt Molly, and he sent word that he would come to visit next Thursday. He wanted to talk to Mrs. Davidson about the boys. Molly told the nine boys that they would have to wear their best suits and be very polite to the Rabbi when he arrived.

They protested.

"That's not our problem," Kenneth, the oldest, said. "Michael and Robert and me are Baptists. The Rabbi doesn't want to see us."

"And we," said Victor, "don't want to see him."

"But you are Jewish," said Aunt Molly.

"So what?" retorted Victor. "Jonas, Isadore, Irwin, and Donald and me can be Jewish without a Rabbi."

Douglas, the Episcopalian, spoke up: "Aunt Molly, if you allow the Rabbi to come, you'll have to let the Baptist minister come to see you and, Aunt Molly, you couldn't stand him. He's a bore. And if my minister hears about this, maybe he will want to come, and I don't want him here. He doesn't like me. He says I ask too many questions. Anyhow, why do we have to be here? We aren't Jews."

Aunt Molly surveyed her brood. "I don't know about Episcopalians and Baptists, but it won't hurt you to stay for the Rabbi's visit. That's the way it's done in polite society. You want for the Rabbi to think this house is for the uneducated and that he should take you away to an orphan asylum?" That did it. Seeing the Rabbi was a small price to pay for staying with Aunt Molly.

So it was arranged, with the boys grumbling. The Rabbi was to come the following week. Aunt Molly told my mother, "I should bring them up like heathens? And it won't hurt the four Gentile boys to get a little Jewish."

"Well," my mother said scornfully, "What about the Jewish boys getting a little Gentile influence?"

Molly shook her head. "It won't take with them. You know how stubborn Jews are. Gentiles have been trying for years to do this, and Sol's boys have too much of Sol in them. But I don't want the neighbors to talk, so I'll have all nine boys there and I'll give the Rabbi some tea and I'll wear my new black dress and the boys will wear their best suits and the Rabbi will know they are nice boys."

But Aunt Molly had reckoned without her boys. They had watched Molly in her various moods and had taken on some of her courage and originality. Douglas talked to Reverend Longworth, his Episcopal minister, and explained that the Rabbi of his foster brothers' Temple was coming to their house and he thought it would be nice if the minister would come to see Aunt Molly, too. Would he stop in to see them? He explained that they were all adopted by Aunt Molly. The minister was interested. He thought he might. When would be a good time? "What about next Thursday?" said Douglas.

That Sunday, Reverend Thompson, the Baptist minister, decided that it was time he visited Michael, Kenneth and Robert. He had heard that they had been adopted by a Mrs. Davidson, a Jewish lady, and this worried him. As fate, which occasionally has a wry sense of humor, would have it he chose Thursday to make the visit.

Thursday arrived. The boys were dressed up in their best. Molly wore her black dress, and the teapot was ready. The dining room table was set with Molly's best cloth, which had been a wedding present for her marriage to Sol. The boys were warned to be careful and not spill anything or the Rabbi would think they had no manners, and if they had no manners, the Rabbi would be certain that she, Aunt Molly, was at fault.

"Don't worry," said Victor. "Once he meets you, he won't notice us."

Molly was nervous. The boys were fidgety—particularly Douglas, because he knew what Aunt Molly didn't know: that the Episcopal minister was coming too. The bell rang and Molly ushered in Rabbi Kantrovitz. The Rabbi smiled as Aunt Molly introduced Al's boy, Bill's three sons and Sol's five.

"Oh, yes," said the Rabbi. "I know Sol's sons." And with a gleam in his eyes, he turned to Aunt Molly and said, "Are the other four boys going to be converts to Judaism?"

Aunt Molly rolled her lovely eyes in shock. "Rabbi, my husbands Al and Bill would turn in their graves at such an idea."

Michael whispered to Robert, "Now she's turning them in their graves. Whenever she says that, she's getting stubborn. You can't argue with her when she says that."

"Well," the Rabbi said to Aunt Molly, "that's not why I am here. I came to talk to you about something else."

But before the Rabbi had a chance to tell her, the doorbell rang.

"Let me go." Douglas jumped up, ran to the door and welcomed the Reverend Longworth.

"Aunt Molly," Douglas said, "this is the Episcopal minister of the church you send me to." (Was this his revenge for having to go to church?)

Aunt Molly shook hands with the Reverend Longworth, then asked Michael, who was now seven years of age, to put another cup on the table, then again introduced the boys. They solemnly rose from their

31

chairs and shook hands with the Reverend. (Aunt Molly had tried to drill them in etiquette; they were to stand and bow, she had said. "Not bow," said Michael, "that's silly. We're not Lord Fauntleroys." "Well, then," Aunt Molly said, accepting the correction, "shake hands.")

"Why don't we sit down for a cup of tea?" Aunt Molly suggested now.

"Aunt Molly," said Michael, "Reverend Longworth isn't Jewish. He doesn't drink tea."

"Michael, I know. Your father wasn't Jewish and he drank only coffee, so go out in the kitchen and make some coffee."

"No, no," protested the Reverend. "Tea will do. One of my grandfathers was English, and he always drank tea."

The Rabbi laughed. "If you don't mind, make me a cup of coffee. I hate tea."

Aunt Molly shrugged. "Rabbi, you must be partly Gentile if you prefer coffee."

"That's right," said the Rabbi, "and if Reverend Longworth prefers tea, he must be a little Jewish."

This pleased Aunt Molly, who by conviction was neither Jewish nor Episcopalian. She had her own relationship with God, who, she privately believed, looked upon Episcopalians, Catholics, Jews, Baptists, Methodists—all of them as though they were clubs with different memberships. God was God, who had no time for clubs even if they were churches.

But the doorbell now rang again, and it was none other than the Baptist minister, Reverend Thompson. His entrance upset even Aunt Molly. The boys were bewildered. How could all of this happen on one night? Aunt Molly recovered sufficiently to welcome the Reverend Thompson.

"Come sit at the table," she said. "What would you like, tea or coffee?"

The Reverend shuddered. "No tea or coffee. Could I have a little hot chocolate?"

There was no chocolate in the house. Molly looked unhappy, but Robert and Michael jumped up. "We'll get it, Aunt Molly."

Aunt Molly rolled her eyes in despair. The Reverend Thompson said he was sorry to cause any trouble. He had just dropped in to see her and welcome her to his church.

Reverend Longworth laughed. "That's why I'm here."

"Well," said the Rabbi, "I have to admit that this is an unusual situation." Although five of the boys attended his Temple, their aunt never came, he pointed out. There was silence for a moment, and then Aunt Molly smiled her encouraging smile and said, "Rabbi, how could I do that? Do I want to hurt my Episcopalian son or my three Baptist boys? God will understand, Rabbi—it's enough that the boys go to Temple. And to tell you the truth, Rabbi, I make them go. Why should I give the neighbors anything to talk about? The boys will go to the church that their fathers belonged to. I moved to this neighborhood after I sold Bill's house so the boys would be near a Temple and the Baptist church. Douglas gets carfare because the Episcopal church is far away. But to tell you the truth, Reverend Longworth, I think he should go to the Baptist church because it's closer. Would we hurt your feelings if he transfers to Reverend Thompson's?

It's nothing against the Episcopalians. It's just that the church is so far away."

Up spoke Douglas. "Why can't I go to the Rabbi's Temple—it's even closer."

"Only Jews come to my Temple," said Rabbi Kantrovitz. "I don't think you would want to come."

"Why not?" said Douglas, who had a stubborn streak. "Aunt Molly is Jewish. If it's all right for her, why isn't it for me?"

The Rabbi was saved answering this question when Robert and Michael came from the kitchen with the chocolate.

So the Rabbi and the Baptist and the Episcopalian minister sat around Aunt Molly's table and learned from her how she had come to adopt the nine boys.

"But, Mrs. Davidson," said Reverend Longworth, "this is a big undertaking. Why didn't their relatives take them when their fathers died?"

"Should I know why?" said Aunt Molly. "They didn't want them. They were going to send them to an orphanage. I knew God didn't want that, so I took them, and they are good boys and they will stay with me."

The Rabbi rose to leave. "Mrs. Davidson, God has blessed this house. May it prosper and let the light of God shine upon it."

Then the Reverend Thompson raised his hand, "May the blessing of the Lord rest upon these children."

And then the Reverend Longworth, tall and lanky and young, took Aunt Molly's hand. "Whatever church you belong to will be holier because you are there."

The three men left and Aunt Molly was crying. The

boys stood around helplessly. To see Aunt Molly cry was devastating. Aunt Molly wiped her eyes.

"So," she said as she began clearing the table, "where did you get the chocolate?"

"That," said Robert, "was easy. You know John Farnum?"

"The boy with the red hair?" asked Aunt Molly. "So what has that got to do with chocolate?"

"Well, he's a Baptist, so I figured he'd have some chocolate. He said he wouldn't give it to me, and I told him I'd punch him if he didn't; but he said, 'Go ahead and I'll knock you down the steps.' So I said, 'All right, I won't punch you. Sell me the can.' And I gave him a quarter and I got the chocolate."

Aunt Molly sighed. "And where did you get the quarter?"

"It's the quarter I was supposed to drop in the collection box, but I didn't."

Molly was angry. "Why didn't you?"

"I don't know. I guess God kept me from dropping it in the box. He must have known we didn't have any cocoa."

4

I was going to my first dance, and I would have preferred going to my own hanging. I didn't care about the boy that was to be my escort. He was at least ten inches taller than I.

"How," I protested to my mother, "do you talk to anyone almost a foot taller than you are? My neck will ache trying to look up at him."

Aunt Molly said, "So why look up at him? Let him look down at you. When you do look up at him, be sure and flutter your eyelashes." This technique came easy to Aunt Molly, but I was on the verge of tears.

"I don't know how to flutter my eyelids."

"Try it," urged Aunt Molly. All I achieved was blinking.

"No good," I wailed. "I'm not beautiful like you, and I'll look ridiculous blinking."

Aunt Molly examined me carefully, then turned to my mother and said, "She's like a green pear that's going to be ripe someday."

I giggled. The thought of being a pear enchanted me. "Why not a peach?" I asked.

"No," said Molly, "a peach you'll never be. You're too skinny. But a pear has a nice figure. You'll have a waistline."

"But, Aunt Molly, in a pear the bottom is bigger than the top."

"So, do you want a bust size forty and a tiny bottom? You'll look like Mrs. Fagelstein, who is so big on top that she can't bend over."

"But, Aunt Molly, never mind what I'm going to be like when I'm twenty. I'm sixteen and I'm going out with Sam Hertzbaum and he's six feet tall. How am I going to dance with him? I'll be way below his chin, and he makes me nervous. He just stands there, and I have to do all the talking. He's a big lummox."

"What's so bad about that? I'll tell you, my niece who looks like a green pear. You should know what a woman should do."

I expostulated, "But I'm not a woman yet."

"So write down what I tell you and remember it. A woman until she gets married is a trimming to a man's life; she should talk and say nice things and laugh and smile."

"Oh, yes, with teeth like yours I'd laugh all the time, but mine are crooked."

Aunt Molly waved this aside. "You should also lean slightly on him when you walk with him to make him feel big and strong and protective. You should walk like this." Aunt Molly demonstrated. "Don't walk straight, swish a little. This makes the man feel that you are not a waitress or grocery store clerk but a woman whose business is to be a woman." (A lot Aunt Molly would have cared about the Women's Lib Movement. Men were to be conquered, and Aunt Molly marshaled her assets for conquests as carefully as generals marshal their regiments.)

"What do you mean be a woman? What else can a female be?"

Aunt Molly looked at me sternly. "To be a woman means that you are different than a man. A man walks straight to get from one place to another—straight like a streetcar—but a woman must undulate to reveal that with a woman there are pleasures."

"What pleasures can I give a man?"

"Not yet. You are still a pear," my mother said. "According to your Aunt Molly."

My aunt ignored the interruption and went on. "A man works all day, and when he takes a girl or a woman out, it's because he's ready to enjoy life. He wants to laugh and to look at something pretty, and you must smell nice. When a man dances with a woman, he should feel that he is holding a rose."

"All right," said my mother. "First she looks like a pear, but now a rose too?"

"Did I say she should be like a rose? She should smell like a rose," and Molly waved her perfumed handkerchief.

"Why do I have to smell like a rose? Why doesn't Sam Hertzbaum have to smell like a rose?"

"Because he's a man. Men don't have to smell like flowers. They just have to smell clean. I told you, women are supposed to be trimmings."

"Fine trimmings," snorted my mother. "How can you smell like a rose when you have to scrub floors and chop herring? So you are so smart, you tell me."

"Did I say you are trimmings after you are married? I said when you go out with a boy, when you don't have to chop herring or scrub floors. After you are married, that's different."

"Well, Aunt Molly, you say smell like a rose in order to get him to marry you, and then you become a dandelion washing, ironing and cooking. Is that what you mean?"

Before Molly could answer, my mother scornfully said, "So how should my sister, Molly, know about scrubbing and washing? She's a trimming before and after the wedding."

"That's right," said Aunt Molly. "When you get married, if you're smart you smell like a rose and a carnation, and if you smell like a violet too, you don't wash or scrub or iron."

My mother exploded. "So you become a garden after you're married!"

"Why not?" said Aunt Molly. "Why should I scrub?"

I objected. "Look, I'm not getting married to Sam, I'm just going to a dance with him; and I'm worried what I should talk about to him. He's so dumb."

"He is not dumb," Aunt Molly told me. "Can he write? Can he open an umbrella if it rains? Does he know about George Washington? Does he know how to use a telephone?" Without waiting for an answer, Aunt Molly added, "So he is not dumb."

"What am I supposed to do? Talk to him about George Washington and umbrellas? What kind of conversation is that?"

"You should listen to me. Everybody is interested in something. Tell him how handsome he looks when he's dancing; ask him if his mother makes good chicken soup. To tell you the truth, I often don't listen to what the man I'm with is saying. I'm thinking of something else, but I smile and that works."

"Aunt Molly, you mean if I smile and roll my eyes and swish as I walk and smell like a rose, I'll be a winner?"

"Why not? It works for me."

"Doesn't it wear you down swishing and smiling?"

"Why should a man go out with a woman and pay for her dinner unless she returns it with a few smiles? Does it hurt to smile and be friendly? How much does it cost? Does it hurt you to smile? No. Sometimes I enjoy it. I'm going out with a builder, and I went to the library and read about buildings in the encyclopedia so I should know what he is talking about when he tells me about mortgages, architects and blueprints. Do you know that he builds by following lines, and he makes a lot of money?"

"So for him," my mother said, "you are a rose, a carnation and a violet maybe?"

"I like him," Molly said dreamily.

"So you'll go around with him, and maybe he'll give you one of those houses he builds with lines."

"What's his name?" I asked.

"Francesconio."

"What kind of name is that?"

"What do you mean what kind of name is that? It's an Italian name. It's as good as Goldberg or Fine or Schwartz."

"Vey is mir. Molly, a Baptist, an Episcopalian and now a Catholic."

"So what have you got against a Catholic?"

"He's a shaygets, and you should marry another shaygets?"

"No more marriages," said Molly. "No more ever."

"Well, I'm glad that's settled," I said, "but I still don't want to go out with Sam, because I can't talk with him."

Aunt Molly, however, was now thinking of her Italian, but before she left to meet him, Aunt Molly with her generous heart gave me her bottle of rose perfume with which to win Sam Hertzbaum.

5

Molly was really a woman of means—after all, she had come into $16,500 from her three husbands. But there were the nine boys, so she needed more money. With her beautiful figure and white throat and auburn hair and violet-blue eyes, she was a decoration anywhere. No more factories for her. She wanted a job, she explained, where she could dress every day as befitted a widow who was not penniless. One look at her beautiful face and smile and she was hired as a model. The store's publicity department recognized that Molly was a knockout and would bring customers into the store.

This, she explained to my mother, was because she needed the forty-four dollars a week for food for the boys. Her $16,500 was spent mostly on the house she had moved into.

"So," said my mother disapprovingly, "forty-four dollars a week for nine boys. Who told you you should take care of them? Let them go to their uncles or the orphanage."

Molly brushed aside my mother's lament. She had heard it before.

"What will you do with Michael, the youngest one? At least send him to the orphanage."

Aunt Molly had her own stubbornness. "Bertha,"

she said accusingly, "if, God forbid, your children were left orphans, would you want yours to go to an orphan asylum and a Baptist orphanage? Who knows what they would give him to eat? Who would wash his ears?"

My mother was apoplectic. "Do you need the President of the United States to wash his ears? What kind of craziness is that? So, you can go once a week to the orphanage and wash his ears."

Aunt Molly was shaken. Who would take care of Michael while she worked? Could Bertha, she asked, take care of him during the day?

My mother promptly answered no, that she had enough to do to take care of her house and her children. She should bring a Baptist into her family? No, if Aunt Molly wanted to be crazy, let her be. But not Bertha.

So Aunt Molly called all the boys and told them that Michael would have to go to the orphanage. There was silence and Michael, too young to understand what it meant, asked, "Are all of you coming with me?"

The boys were silent. Michael looked around and turned to Aunt Molly, "I don't want to go if they're not coming."

"So, what should I do? Take you to work with me?"

"Yes, I'd like that, Aunt Molly."

Robert looked up and snapped. "Don't be silly. What would Aunt Molly do with you all day?"

"She doesn't have to do anything. I'll take my marbles to the store and play with them there."

"All day? You're cracked. No one plays marbles all day. And what are you going to do—play marbles with yourself?"

"Sure, why not? I'll play at one end, and then I'll

move over to the other side and shoot from that end. It's a great game because then I win even if I lose."

Molly listened to this dialogue. "Michael, you sound like a Talmudic scholar the way you argue."

"What's a Talmudic scholar?"

"You should know," Aunt Molly told him, "because a Talmudic scholar is a man who sits with other men figuring out what God thinks and what Moses heard when God spoke to him. They are good men, and the more they study and argue, the wiser they become."

"Don't they do any work? Who feeds them??

"What silly questions you ask," said Irwin, who was listening to the conversation.

"That's not a silly question," Michael maintained. "Is it, Aunt Molly?"

"These men, you dope," Irwin told him, "are fed and supported by their families."

"What for," said Michael, "just so they can think? Gosh, I do that all the time—even while I'm shooting marbles. Why can't they work and think at the same time?"

"Probably God wouldn't like it if they worked while they were thinking about His laws. He wouldn't want anything to interfere while they concentrated on Him," Molly told him. Douglas was listening and asserted triumphantly: "I told you I didn't believe in God. He's silly."

"Douglas, a young boy should not say such things. Who do you think made the world?"

"Well, if He made the world, why does He need those guys to sit around and tell people what God wants? Can't He tell us Himself?"

"You know what, Douglas?" expostulated Irwin. "With your strange beliefs, you should have to go to Sunday school every day, not only once a week. If God is good enough for everyone else, why isn't He for you?"

Aunt Molly interrupted. "So you don't believe in God, but the question is, What should I do with Michael?"

"Nothing, Aunt Molly. Don't you worry. When Mrs. Kolensky comes to clean in the mornings, she can make my lunch."

"And you'll tell her not to believe in God because Douglas doesn't so she'll leave and tell everybody that Douglas, aged eleven, has denounced God," said Irwin sarcastically.

"All right, Aunt Molly, I promise I won't say a word about God to Mrs. Kolensky so she won't think this is a Godless house."

"Well, that will be a miracle in itself," said Irwin. "That ought to persuade you that miracles do exist."

6

Mrs. Kolensky worked for Molly. She ran the house because Molly as a model made enough money at the department store to pay Mrs. Kolensky twelve dollars a week. Mrs. Kolensky always wore a white apron heavily starched, so starched that it stood out away from her body and made a crackling sound as she walked. The boys called her "Crackie" but never to her face.

She had a harassed and worried look and rarely smiled. Life, she insisted, was a vale of tears, so why should she smile. She would read with relish any item in the newspaper describing an accident. It proved her conviction that all of life was a hazard. She wore glasses that were always on the tip of her nose. Since there was a crack in one of the lenses, she, obviously, didn't need them. Irwin said she wore them because she believed they made her look impressive.

Her three sons were married and lived in different cities and dutifully wrote to her every month. Her husband was dead. She was really lonely, so she transferred her affection to Molly and the boys. She was conscientious and felt responsible for the boys, though she always acted as though they were a burden.

"You should know, Mrs. Davidson," she said. "I have three children—may God keep them—but they are married and they live their lives and I live mine, but since I came here I now live nine more lives. I worry about Robert—his socks are always falling down —and Kenneth doesn't brush his teeth and Irwin forgets to take his bath and Douglas has his head stuck in a book and Robert broke his glasses. Maybe you should stay home and take care of them."

"Oh, come on, Mrs. Kolensky," said Kenneth. "You know Aunt Molly has to work and you know Robert will get a new pair and if Douglas doesn't take his bath on Tuesday he'll take it on Wednesday."

"Nix on that," spoke up Victor. "Wednesday's my night."

"So," said Mrs. Kolensky, "you see first I had three to worry about but now I have nine, so I'm quitting."

Michael put his arms around Mrs. Kolensky's waist. "You'll miss us. And if you don't leave, Kenneth will brush his teeth and Douglas won't read at the table."

"I make good gefilte fish, and Douglas doesn't know what he is eating with his nose in his book. What kind of eating is that?"

"Awww, come on, Mrs. Kolensky," interrupted Kenneth, "we'll help with the dishes and we love you."

"Love," snorted Mrs. Kolensky. "You should better brush your teeth. Three I have and now nine more. I should live so long. I worry too much."

"But we do love you, all of us, don't we?" said Douglas. "And I won't read when you cook something special. How could we get along without you? Come on, Mrs. Kolensky, don't make us unhappy. Who would get our breakfast?"

"For a boy as big as you, you should make your own breakfast."

"All right, Mrs. Kolensky, if we make our own breakfast, will you stay?"

So Mrs. Kolensky agreed to remain, and the boys were to discover that every so often she would threaten to leave and had to be persuaded to remain. The truth was that Mrs. Kolensky wouldn't leave. The house was home to her, and she both scolded and babied the boys, and they very early recognized that scold though she might, there was nothing she wouldn't do for them. But how she could scold! There were fights at the school, and every so often one of the boys would come home with a black eye or a scratch or a bloody nose.

It was Mrs. Kolensky who applied ice or the bandage, but always with a running commentary: "Nice boys don't fight. What will Aunt Molly say? My boys never had fights. What will your minister say? And do you think stockings grow on trees? Do you know how much they cost? Where were all your adopted brothers? What kind of boys are they that they let you get a bloody nose and a scratched knee?" This harangue occurred one afternoon when Douglas came home with a bloody nose.

"I don't need my brothers. I'll take care of my own fights," Douglas told her.

But Mrs. Kolensky was in readiness when the older boys came home. "So what kind of children are you to run away and let your little brother get a bloody nose? Fine brothers! You should be ashamed!"

Aunt Molly arrived at this moment and took Douglas to her arms and kissed him. Then Douglas broke down and sobbed as he told Aunt Molly about the gang that attacked him. Aunt Molly turned to the other boys.

"What's up, Aunt Molly? What happened to Douglas?" they demanded.

Mrs. Kolensky had her two cents' worth, and she expressed it. "What happened to such a nice Episcopalian?" and then she exploded: "Fine brothers you are!"

"Hold on, hold on! What's this all about? We don't know anything about this."

So Douglas told Irwin how a gang surrounded him on the playground and tried to get his marbles, so he punched one of them and that's what started it.

"Why did you punch him?"

"The marbles are mine. They have no right to them."

Property rights are part of our philosophy, and Douglas was expressing it vehemently and quite logically.

"So," said Mrs. Kolensky, "were a few marbles worth a bloody nose and torn stockings?"

"You bet," said Irwin. "Let those stinkers"—even Aunt Molly didn't comment about the word "stinkers" "—get away with this and next they'll take something else. Let's gang up on them, and that will stop it."

"Let's take an oath," said Michael, "like the knights of old: 'One for all and all for one.' Then no one will ever touch one of us."

Aunt Molly looked perplexed. "You tell me, Kenneth—you're the oldest. What is this 'One for all and all for one'?"

"From now on, Aunt Molly, we will be known as the Davidson gang, and if they bother Douglas or any one of us, the whole gang of us will attack them."

"But I don't want for you to be fighters. I want you

48

to be learners to learn at school so you can all go to college."

"Don't worry, Aunt Molly—if they know there's a Davidson gang" (that was Molly's married name and that was how the boys were referred to, though they kept their fathers' names), "they won't start anything. We'll fix them."

That's actually the way it worked out. A few days after that the same gang approached Douglas and began taunting him. To their surprise Douglas, instead of running, told them to shut up. When they began crowding him, Irwin and Isadore and Victor and Kenneth—all of them came running and dared them to touch Douglas.

This demonstrated a theory that was to evolve in our decade. Each country loads itself with armament so deadly that no one dares start a war. If God moves in mysterious ways His wonders to perform, it may well be that a warless world will be the result of the deadliness of modern weapons.

And for Molly's boys it was the beginning of a relationship of solidarity that lasted all through their lives.

Irwin and Isadore were the first two to finish college. Kenneth was taking a year off to work on a thesis he was preparing. They helped Douglas, who in turn helped the younger ones. The loyalty among the nine was amazing. It was the result of Molly's philosophy. They were orphans—she was in place of their mothers and fathers. If they did anything wrong, she told them people would say it was because she didn't know how to bring them up. They had to stand by her and prove that she was right in keeping them with her instead of sending them to an orphan asylum.

Each one of the boys in his own way wanted to please Molly. She was warmhearted and showed them great affection. No boy left the house without kissing her good-bye. When they had a sore throat or a broken leg, it was Molly who would sit next to their bed and feed them and hold their hand. Molly was generous in her expression of affection. Her tenderness won their loyalty and devotion. They adored her, and not one of them would do anything that would make her unhappy.

It's true they agreed she had some silly notions—like insisting they all go to Sunday school. And there was one ritual they all detested, but Molly was adamant; every Sunday before they left for Sunday school, Molly would spray each of their handkerchiefs with a perfume.

"But, Aunt Molly, that's only for sissies," the boys would protest.

"Sissies, shmissies" was Aunt Molly's answer. "You want that your Rabbi and minister should say you smell bad?"

"But, Molly, my minister doesn't sniff me. He doesn't come near me. I don't know if he knows I'm there."

"Some minister you got. My minister said, 'Um.' You know how he says 'Um' from deep down in his throat—maybe it comes all the way from his stomach. Anyway, he says, 'Um, someone smells nice.' I quickly put the handkerchief in my pants pocket so no one would know the perfume came from me."

They argued with her. Kenneth said, "Aunt Molly, I'm a boy, and boys don't smell like flowers."

"So you want to smell like a dandelion? Not my boys!"

So Molly went on perfuming their handkerchiefs and as soon as the boys were out of the house they took out the handkerchiefs and flopped them in the wind. Anyone who had been watching would have wondered why the Davidson boys waved their handkerchiefs every Sunday.

Throughout their lives the perfume of carnations brought back the memory of the Sunday mornings and their perfumed handkerchiefs. And they never neglected to send carnations to Molly on her birthday when they were grown and could afford it.

7

The department store that hired Molly was a large store, and Molly was fascinated by the way it was managed. Since she was outgoing, she made friends easily. The other model, Cynthia Parker, introduced her to various clerks, and Molly was drawn to a gentle, sweet, and pretty clerk in the underwear department, Alice Richards. Alice was frail and ethereal-looking, and everyone in the store knew that she was in love with Mr. Phillips, the general manager, who everyone also knew was torn between devotion to Alice and Cynthia. Bets were that Cynthia would win out.

Alice invited Molly to her home. Alice lived in a quaint house that had been converted from a store into a six-room dwelling. She lived with her old father, who constantly said, "Ahum, Ahum," starting every sentence that way and ending with the same sound. He seemed to be as frail and gentle as Alice. For Molly this was a great change from her boisterous home with the nine boys running in and out.

Alice admitted to Molly that she was in love with Mr. Phillips, but she was sure that he was interested in Cynthia.

Did Molly like poetry? No one had ever asked Molly such a question.

"What is poetry good for?" she demanded of Alice. "Will it get you Mr. Phillips?"

"I don't know, but I sent him this poem. Do you think he will understand it? It's by Elizabeth Browning."

"Who is she?" asked Molly. "Do you know her? Where does she live?"

So Alice told Molly about the Browning love affair, that Elizabeth Barrett was sickly and spent most of her time on a couch, that she and Robert Browning eloped, and that to tell him how much she loved him she wrote sonnets. "This is one of them," said Alice. "May I read it to you?"

> "I love thee freely, as men strive for right.
> I love thee purely, as they turn from praise.
> I love thee with the passion put to use
> In my old griefs, and with my childhood faiths.
> I love thee with the love I seemed to lose
> With my lost saints—I love thee with the breath,
> Smiles, tears, of all my life!—and, if God choose,
> I shall but love thee better after death."

"Very pretty," said Molly, "but do you think you should send him a poem about saints and a sickly woman? What kind of an approach is this? Why should he like a poem about a woman who is sick and has a backache? What kind of love is that? Why don't you just go up to his office and tell the secretary to go out and leave you alone with him and you tell him that you love him? Why do you have to tell him about this Browning woman? What's that got to do with you? What kind of love is that?"

"Oh, Molly, I just couldn't tell him outright that I'm in love with him. How would that look?"

"You think it is maybe better if this sick woman tells him she loved Robert and that's how he would know you love him?"

This baffled Molly. She certainly would never need a woman who was dead—and who was sickly while she was alive—to do her wooing. Molly's method was purely that of a huckster. She displayed her wares—her beauty and her great smile. She didn't need a go-between.

But that night she discussed poetry with the boys. Did they have it at school?

"Sure," said Kenneth. "I like poetry. It's like singing:

> "By the shores of Gitchee Gumee,
> By the shining Big Sea Water,
> Stood the wigwam of Nokomis,
> Daughter of the Moon, Nokomis."

"That's silly when you think about it," said Irwin. "Why couldn't you just write: 'A dame lived in a house on the edge of a river'?"

"And what about: 'My country, 'tis of thee,/Sweet land of liberty,/Of thee I sing'?" asked Douglas.

"Isn't that silly? Why do they have to mix everything up in poetry? Why can't they say: 'I'd like to sing a song about my country, U.S. of America'?"

"You dumbbells! That's the whole ball of wax about poetry. You got to say it so it's difficult to understand. But Aunt Molly, you know there's poetry in the Bible, and it's love poetry," Irwin said.

"Who makes love in the Bible?" Molly was disturbed. Somehow it didn't seem right to talk about love affairs to God. "Show me, Irwin, where it says about a love affair in the Bible."

"The Rabbi read it to us."

"What kind of Sunday school is it where the Rabbi reads love poems?"

"I told you," said Douglas, "not to send me to Sunday school. Now you'll believe me when I tell you it's all a waste of time, and so is the quarter I have to drop in the box every Sunday."

Molly ignored Douglas and persisted. "Find me what the Rabbi read to you, Irwin."

So Irwin brought the Bible to the dining-room table and began to read:

> "Behold, thou art fair, my love;
>   Thou hast doves' eyes within thy locks.
>   Thy hair is as a flock of goats that appear from
>   Mount Gilead
>   Thy teeth are like a flock of sheep."

"Are you telling me," said Douglas, "that a dame is beautiful if she has hair like a goat and teeth like a sheep?"

"What do you know about a beautiful woman?"

"Well," said Michael, "I think Aunt Molly is beautiful, and she doesn't have eyes like a dove. I know. I've looked at a dove."

But Molly was intrigued. "Read me some more," she directed Irwin.

> "Rise up, my love, my fair one, and come away.
>   For, lo, the winter is past, the rain is over and
>   gone;

The flowers appear on the earth; the time of the
   singing of birds is come,
And the voice of the turtle is heard in our land.
The fig tree putteth forth her green figs,
And the vines with the tender grapes give a good
   smell.
Arise, my love, my fair one, and come away."

Robert broke in. "Who's telling her to get up all
the time? Can't she get up alone? Does someone always
have to wake her?"

"Maybe she likes to sleep a lot," said Michael.

"Who wants her to get up?"

Patiently, Irwin said, "It's King Solomon who wants
her to get up and go someplace with him."

"So why doesn't she get up and go? Maybe Solomon
wanted her to smell the grapes," said Kenneth.

"Who is this guy Solomon?" Kenneth inquired.

"He was king of the Jews."

"Funny kind of a king," put in Michael. "You can
just bet the Baptists don't have a king who yearns for
a babe with eyes like a dove. And he wants her to go
away with him because the grapes give a good smell.
He must be nuts."

"Well, where do you want him to go? To the
movies?"

"Don't be silly. There weren't any in those days;
there sure wasn't much to do."

"Well, he had three hundred wives. That would
keep him busy."

"What did he do when he had company? How did
he introduce them? Meet my wife, Mrs. Solomon
Number One and then Mrs. Solomon Number Two.

How long did it take to introduce them all?" interrupted Robert.

"You're a dope. Kings don't have to introduce their wives," answered Kenneth.

Molly was further intrigued. Maybe there was something to this poetry. Maybe Alice was right in sending the sonnet to Mr. Phillips, but Alice should have put a postscript on the letter with the poem: "Dear Mr. Phillips—But I am very healthy."

She looked around at the boys, and her eyes filled with tears. They were good boys, and they were smart boys. Their fathers, if they had lived, would have been proud of them. And her sister, Bertha, wanted her to put them in an orphan asylum. Never! They knew about poetry;—like Irwin, who could go to the Bible and read her something she never knew.

She would have to tell Alice about Bible poetry and help her get Mr. Phillips. If Alice wanted to tell Mr. Phillips that she loved him, why didn't she send him some strong poetry like: "Rise up, my love . . . and come away." That's the kind of poetry a man would understand.

8

Alice was influenced by Molly. Maybe Molly was right. Perhaps she was too timid. But how could she march up to Mr. Phillips' office and let him know how she felt? She just couldn't do it. Alice was a tiny woman, about five feet one and less than a hundred pounds. Very petite and pretty in a fragile way. She apparently had very little energy and found the hours she spent behind the counter very fatiguing.

Her parents were gentile, very Victorian, and had brought her up to become what they considered a real lady, which in the early 1900s meant that she was full of Victorian inhibitions. Her father had been a teacher and lived on a very small income. He was completely devoted to Alice; she was his whole life. Her mother had died some years ago, and Alice felt very much responsible for her father.

Molly invited her to meet the boys, and they dubbed her the "doll lady" because she was so small. From Alice, Molly learned many things; for Alice read a great deal and loved to tell Molly about her books and the ideas and philosophies of the authors. Molly's interests were mostly about personal matters.

Molly wanted to know how Mr. Phillips had become

so important to Alice. "Well," Alice told her, "when I applied for the job, Mr. Phillips took me out for lunch and explained what I would have to do if I wanted to become a buyer, and after that he would stop at my department to see how I was getting along, and sometimes he takes me home. And," continued Alice, looking around to be sure no one overheard her, "he kissed me and tonight I'm going out for dinner with him. I'm so excited, Molly, I can hardly wait until seven o'clock, and he has a beautiful car. Sometimes when I'm sitting next to him I just wish we would go driving on and on forever so I could be with him and belong to him."

"What do you mean, belong to him? What are you —a house? a coat? an automobile? What kind of foolishness is that?"

In the ensuing weeks it seemed to Molly that Alice was getting thinner, and she coughed a good deal. A number of times she was not well enough to come to work. Molly went to see her.

"Molly," Alice told her, "I'm getting like Elizabeth Barrett Browning. I'm lying on the couch a lot. It's an effort to get up. I hope I won't have to quit my job. We can use the money because my father has only a small income. We can get along, but my check helps. But if I'm sick, I won't see Mr. Phillips, and I'm miserable when I don't see him."

Molly knew that Alice had reason to worry, because Cynthia told her that Mr. Phillips now dated her a lot.

"Is he going to marry you?" she asked Cynthia.

Cynthia laughed. "Not if I have anything to do with it. He's not rich enough for me. He's way down on the list of possibilities."

"What do you mean, down on the list? Then you don't want Mr. Phillips?"

"Nohow—only to pay for my dinner."

Molly was fascinated. It had never occurred to her to use a man's attention as a money-saving scheme.

"It's simple, Molly. I go out for dinner with Mr. Phillips because every time I don't have to buy my dinner I put the amount it would have cost me into my savings account. I'm saving money to go to New York and get a model's job there because that's where they pay big money."

"But you go out practically every night with some man or other."

"Sure, and my bank account is getting bigger. But don't think it's easy. Lot of times I'm bored, and then some of them are wolves and there's always the struggle at the door to get them to leave. Sometimes I think I can't stand them fighting to get a kiss, but then I think of New York and I go out again the next night.

"You see, being a model gives men all sorts of ideas. They think they've got to buy us dinner and give us gifts. You ought to try it sometimes. You'll have no trouble. You are more beautiful than I am, but you must learn to dress with more dash. You know you can buy any of the clothes we model at cost. Like this hat with the plumes. Isn't it smashing? Try it on. Molly, see how beautiful your hair is against the velvet and black plumes? You're a real knockout."

"But," said Aunt Molly, "I don't want to go out for dinner with someone I don't like."

"Well," said Cynthia, who was a realist, "then you will have to pay for your own dinners, and your savings account won't be as big as mine."

Molly went back to her original question. "Then you don't really want Mr. Phillips?"

"No, I just told you. He is a nice man, but he doesn't mean anything to me. Why? Do you want him?"

Of course Mr. Phillips was unaware that Molly and Cynthia were directing his fate.

"No, I don't want him, but Alice does, and you know, Cynthia, my heart hurts for her, and besides she is so sickly. I don't think she will come back to work. She doesn't have the strength. You know she sends Mr. Phillips poems about other sick women?"

"Poems about sick women?"

"Yes, she does, and to me that is not good. She should, I told her, send him poems about healthy women."

"Well, has she?"

"I don't know if there are poems about healthy women."

"But, tell me, how sick is Alice?"

"Her father told me she is anemic, but I think it's because of Mr. Phillips."

Molly, being tenderhearted, had told Alice that Mr. Phillips had asked about her and would be stopping in to see her. Having assured Alice that Mr. Phillips would come to see her, Molly was obliged to make good on her assurance to Alice, who was quivering with delight at the thought that Mr. Phillips would stop to see her.

It was no problem for Molly. She was direct where matters of the heart were concerned. It was a simple equation. Alice was in love with Mr. Phillips; Mr. Phillips was free, so why shouldn't he make Alice happy? Someone would have to tell him that this was the only way Alice would get better. So Molly appeared in Mr. Phillips' office.

"Yes," said Mr. Phillips, "what can we do for you, Mrs. Davidson? The sales of the dresses you model are very satisfactory. Is there something wrong? Is the dressing room too small? Don't you have enough time to change costumes?"

"No, no, there is nothing the matter. I want for you to know about Alice."

Mr. Phillips looked perplexed, "What about Alice?"

"Well, Mr. Phillips, Alice, do you know, loves you very much. She writes poetry to you. Do you know she went to college? She's very cultivated."

Mr. Phillips looked perplexed. "What do you want me to do about it? Although I don't think it's any of your business."

"I know, Mr. Phillips, that I should not say anything, but for me love is beautiful and you shouldn't throw it away. It's valuable."

The manager didn't know whether to be angry or amused. Mrs. Davidson was certainly interfering in matters that were none of her business. So, almost speechless, he stared at Molly.

Molly sat down even though she had not been invited to. "You see," she said, "Alice is very sick. She has only her father, who can't say anything without an 'ahum.' Her mother is dead and I'm her friend, and I don't think she is ever going to get better."

"Why are you telling me all this?"

"I thought if you could make believe for a short time that you love her it would help to get her better. If she does get better, maybe you'll learn to love her, and if you don't, then she will be strong enough to face that fact. But in the meantime, what can it hurt you to lie a little? It will be a *mitzvah*."

Mr. Phillips raised his eyebrows.

"A mitzvah," Molly told him, "is a good deed, and it counts when God figures out what you have done in life. And if you're not Jewish, don't let that worry you, because God doesn't have time to figure out what church you belong to. It's all the same to Him. In my house my boys are Jewish, Episcopalian, and Baptist, and God treats them all the same way."

Mr. Phillips gulped. His new model seemed to be on intimate terms with God's philosophy.

"Just what did you tell Alice?"

"So what did I tell her? I said you asked me how she was, and I said you were coming to see her. Her cheeks got real pink, and she said, 'Molly, really, or are you making it up?' So if you don't go, she'll know I was sorry for her and lied to her, and she will get worse."

"So you've decided I am to be medicine for Alice?" Mr. Phillips asked.

"So you will be medicine. Is that so bad? Can you buy love? Alice is giving it to you for nothing. So you walk in, Mr. Phillips, and you bend down and kiss her on her cheek, and she'll hold your hand and her poor heart that isn't doing so well will beat with happiness. Could a doctor do that? I should tell you, Mr. Phillips, that if you don't go I can't work for you, because you would be a *momser*."

If Mr. Phillips was astonished earlier in the conversation, he was dumbfounded now. He happened to know the meaning of momser.

"All right, Mrs. Davidson," he said wearily, "I'll stop in to see Alice."

63

Molly reported the conversation to Cynthia, who said, "Molly, you are not to be believed. You said all that to the manager of the store?"

"So," said Molly. "He is a man first and then he's a manager. What man doesn't want to hear that a woman loves him?"

"I'll try that technique someday," said Cynthia, "and see if it works."

Molly shrugged. Maybe Alice would sleep tonight.

And Molly was right. Alice did hold on to Mr. Phillips' hand, and he did come to see her often and arranged to have her enter a sanitarium, to build up her red corpuscles. She went willingly and contentedly because Mr. Phillips had made the arrangements and promised to come see her.

So Molly's formula was accepted by Mr. Phillips. He would help Alice get better; then he could decide whether he really loved her. And sometimes he would gaze curiously at Molly, marveling that she had had the courage to tell him what to do.

But for Molly what she had done wasn't lying. It was just a form of medicine that she had asked Mr. Phillips to administer to Alice. "So why shouldn't a man help a woman?" Molly asked Cynthia. "Isn't that what they are supposed to do?"

Cynthia laughed. "Molly, you helped Alice, but I've lost one of my dinner tickets. Since Mr. Phillips started visiting Alice, he doesn't buy me dinner and my savings account isn't doing as well."

"So," said Aunt Molly, "you come to my house for dinner and meet my boys."

And that's how Cynthia met the nine boys, and practically every one of them fell in love with her:

"She's neat." "She's a winner." "Have her over some more."

Cynthia, who never had any brothers, was overwhelmed. She had known nothing of Molly's private life and was literally awed that Molly looked upon herself as the guardian of the nine boys. It revealed a new dimension to Molly and filled Cynthia with admiration.

The store management became aware that the new model was creating a sensation because of her looks and her friendliness and bringing customers to the store. They engaged in some heavy advertising, showing pictures of their two models, Cynthia and Molly. A newspaper reporter arrived to interview Molly.

"Mrs. Davidson, do you mind telling us how old you are?"

Molly looked astonished. "So why should I mind? I'm twenty-five years old."

"But, Mrs. Davidson, it's been reported that you have nine boys. How could that be?"

"What do you mean, how could that be?"

"But you're so young to have nine boys."

"If God wants to give me nine boys, He knows what He is doing. But a miracle it isn't. I had three husbands."

The reporter thought it was a miracle that any woman so young and beautiful could have nine children, but he wondered why Molly didn't stay with her husbands, why she always left them. He could not imagine that any man could leave her. He would have been astonished to learn that Molly had lost three husbands in the space of five years and that because of this she had developed a real neurosis, being convinced that this was a message from God, so no more marriages for her. In some mysterious fashion she held herself responsible for the boys, so she adopted them.

A few days later Cynthia and Molly's picture appeared in a news article in the paper. Francesconio, a friend of Cynthia's, saw the picture and asked Cynthia about Molly. Was she really so beautiful, and did she really have nine boys?

"Yes to both parts of your question," replied Cynthia. "If you'd like to meet her, take us out for dinner."

And that's how Francesconio met his fate.

9

Francesconio was bewildered. Here he was thirty-six years of age. He had never been in love except briefly with his young wife, and she had lived so short a time after their marriage that their life together now seemed like a dream. At sixteen years of age, he had had to go to confession about his first sex experience. After his wife's death, there were a number of brief love affairs that didn't last long, because he never allowed any woman to distract him from his business. All the girls and women he had known were decorations, trimmings. The main interest of his life was his business, and it paid off.

He figured he was lucky and shrewd. In 1906 he was worth more than a half-million dollars, and he calculated that by 1910 he would be worth close to a million. His two brothers worked with him, but it was he who was adventurous, innovative and courageous. In his first few ventures he proceeded with great caution and prudence. Success gave him courage; courage brought him success, and success feeds on itself. So Francesconio was on his way to further financial achievements.

He bought a fine home for his mother and father

because he said if they had not had the courage and vision to leave Italy, he would still be poor and uneducated. Now he was an American-born citizen and would serve this beautiful America in any way he could. He loved America with the great feeling the immigrants had for this land. He was proud of being an American and gladly and cheerfully gave to numerous causes. He was six feet tall with a strong if not handsome face. He still dreamed of someday sculpting a beautiful figure out of marble—he had never got any further than wood carving. Even so, he had a passion for beauty whether it was a flower or a sunset or a woman.

Molly stunned him. She was his dream of a beautiful woman come true. He could hardly believe that she was real, and he fell wildly, madly in love with her. He was dazzled by her smile, her white neck, her tiny waistline and her eyes. Blue, he said, and like a piece of the sky that had fallen out of the heavens.

Molly laughed when he told her so, and when she laughed, her white teeth added to Francesconio's enchantment, and he wooed her assiduously. He wanted to see her every night, but Aunt Molly said no to that. She had to have her sleep and besides she wanted to be with the boys. When Cynthia had told Francesconio that Molly really had nine boys, he was bewildered. So Molly told him about her three husbands and how she happened to take all the boys and give them a home.

Francesconio stared at Molly. "Nine," he said. "Nine boys. How can you take care of them?"

Molly explained that each of the boys' fathers had left some money, which would see the oldest boy through school, and how she felt that if they hadn't married her, her three husbands wouldn't have died.

"That's nonsense—that's old peasant's talk. Of course they didn't die because they were married to you. They died because they were sick or had an accident. I don't believe in any such stuff. It's an old wives' tale. And Molly, I'm not afraid. I want to marry you. I love you."

Molly put her hand in his. "I love you too, but I can't marry you. I know what would happen."

Francesconio held her hand tightly. "I just won't listen to such nonsense. If you love me, I'm going to put an engagement ring and a wedding band on your finger, and I want to do it right away."

Molly was stubborn. "You can put the ring on my finger, but I won't marry you."

"But, Molly, you just said you love me."

"I do, but I won't marry you—but I will live with you."

Francesconio was aghast. "You will live with me but not marry me. You must be crazy. That would be living in sin."

"So, haven't you lived with any other woman?"

"What's that got to do with it? I didn't love those women. Besides, I didn't live with them. Anyway," Francesconio told her with true male logic, "that's before I met you."

"Please, Francesconio, I don't want any confessions. But this is the way it has to be. I made an agreement with God."

"What do you mean by that? No one talks to God."

"What do you do when you pray? Who are you talking to? You are praying to someone!"

Francesconio was exasperated, but he didn't answer.

"Well, maybe you don't pray right, or you don't understand God, or the Jewish God is different. He makes himself understood."

"Well, how does he talk to you? Are you telling me that God told you not to marry me?"

Aunt Molly put her arms around Francesconio's shoulders. "Francesconio, I love you, and I want to live with you."

Francesconio was beside himself with exasperation. This beautiful woman with a smile like sunshine itself tells him she loves him and will live with him but will not marry him.

He removed Molly's arms and pushed her into a chair. "Now, Molly, I don't want any more nonsense about your arrangements with God. I'm not a fool and neither are you. I want the truth. Is it because I'm Italian? Is it because I'm not a college graduate? Is it because you don't think I have enough money? Go to the bank—they'll tell you I've got enough money so you can live in luxury. Or is it because I've had other women? I want an honest answer, and don't beguile me with your smile and stop kissing my hair. Nothing will help. Jesus, I ask you to marry me, and you say you'll live with me but won't marry me. Either you're crazy or I don't hear well or you are not a decent woman."

Molly stood up with tears in her eyes. "Then go away, Francesconio, if you think I'm not a decent woman."

"Well, what else can I believe? If you love me and you're not married to anyone else, what kind of proposition is this? Have you got a secret life? But I won't live with you, you understand? I want a wife, not someone to sleep with. I always thought Jewish women were good women. Maybe you don't think I'm good enough for a husband. I'm thirty-six years old, and I don't want a playmate—I want a wife and I want children."

So Aunt Molly told Francesconio why she wouldn't marry him.

"But what kind of a deal with God is that?"

But Aunt Molly could not be moved. She was sure that God had made His intentions clear, and this was the way it was. It was not her fault that God's reasons were inscrutable. He did many strange things. Why did He allow the San Francisco earthquake? she demanded to know, and Why did Mrs. O'Leary's cow knock over a lantern and start the Chicago fire?

"But," said Francesconio, "if that is your reason, maybe because I'm a Catholic nothing like those things will happen to me."

Molly wasn't convinced. As far as she was concerned, God wasn't denominational. That wasn't God's doing. If people wanted different forms of prayer, that was all right with God. It was like belonging to different lodges. So Francesconio needn't think that because he was a Catholic, God would make an exception in his case. Did God ever change his mind about the Ten Commandments? Those were his orders, and that's the way it had to be. It was the same with God and her three husbands. One would have to be stupid not to understand.

Francesconio was stunned. This woman, Molly Davidson, whom he loved, was different from anyone else he had ever met.

"Molly, what if we have children?" he asked. "Do you want our children to be illegitimate?"

"Of course not," Molly told him. "It will be very

simple. If we have any children, you can adopt them. That will make them legitimate."

This really stumped Francesconio. Molly had, apparently, figured out all the angles.

"How do I introduce you? As my wife who isn't really married to me?"

"So who will ask? Do you have to give my name and address and history when you introduce me? I will be your wife because I will be living with you."

"Molly, that is insane. You love me, don't you?"

Tears welled up in Molly's lovely blue eyes. This was too much for Francesconio, who yearned for Molly and could not endure to see her weep. He took her into his arms.

"It's crazy, it's insane—but if that's the way you want it, that's the way it will be."

Francesconio walked home that night. There was a beautiful moon, and the lilacs were in bloom—their perfume pervading the air. What a woman, so beautiful and so generous in taking care of nine boys. What a wife she would make. But suddenly he stopped and leaned against a fence. But she wouldn't be his wife. What was he going to do about that? Molly fascinated him. She was a true original, but after all, he had to live in a world of average people and Molly was not average.

He thought of her as she looked in the violet-colored dress with her auburn hair touched with gold. Her skin, he could swear, was as soft as rose petals. Even her earlobes were lovely, like small pearls, and her waistline— He quivered at the memory of what she felt like in his arms.

He yearned for the day when he could unpin her hair and see it fall over her shoulders. He had never before experienced so deep an emotion about any woman.

He broke off a branch of a lilac bush and held it to his face as he continued his walk, briskly now and filled with happiness at the thought that Molly loved him. He thrust aside his disturbed feeling at her refusal to marry him. Somehow he would change her resolution, he was sure, but he didn't know Molly very well. He did not realize what a fixation she suffered from—a belief that marriage was not for her.

Then, of course, there was the problem of his parents—their reaction to a non-Catholic. But that was unimportant. He could win them over, but what to say to his friends. How to explain the lack of a wedding.

But then he remembered Molly's radiant smile when he had put the engagement ring with its brilliant diamond on her finger. Nothing really mattered except that he loved her and she loved him.

He walked along with his bold stride, holding the lilac branch in his hand, whistling happily. A policeman watched him and wondered why this rugged-looking man should be walking along the street at midnight, carrying a lilac branch.

Love, my friend, Francesconio would probably have told him—love and the rapture that goes with it. Love that turns a drab meadow into a flowering orchard; love that envelops the days with radiance; love that makes one for everyone; love that intoxicates the soul and the flesh; love, creation's most generous and gracious gift. It has but to touch one and the world be-

73

comes an enchantment, so Francesconio whistled his happiness while the moon continued to shed its silver light on the earth where love and bitterness, life and death, played out its drama.

10

Francesconio was second generation. His family had left Florence, searching for a land where they would be free of poverty. They landed, as most immigrants did, in New York City. They lived in the ghetto, but they were inured to poverty. That was all they had known in Italy. But America was gleaming with promise—here their sons could climb out of poverty. Here in the New York ghetto Francesconio was born. The family rejoiced. Now they had a son who was a true American by birth, not by naturalization.

By the time Francesconio was in high school, the family had moved to Milwaukee. Francesconio dreamed of being a sculptor, another Michelangelo, but there was no money with which to buy marble, and there were jobs to go to after classes. So he kept his dream to himself and decided to become a builder.

He channeled his creativity into building a house on a side lot that he and one of his brothers had bought with their savings. The house was a success and was sold at a profit, and soon he began to develop a reputation as a builder of quality houses.

When he built the home for his mother and father, he made their dream of America come true. Maybe the streets were not paved with gold, but life in America was beautiful. How could the peasants in Italy have dreamed they would ever have such a home? Francesconio saw his mama and papa's awe as he took them through their new home, and he experienced a warm feeling of happiness that he could bring them such joy. He was a good Catholic and gave generously to his church, but went to confession infrequently.

At twenty-four years of age he was married. Two years later his young wife died in childbirth, and so did the baby. It took him a number of years before he recovered from the shock and began to be interested in women again. His parents tried to introduce him to daughters of some of their friends, but he was in no hurry to marry again. He was having a good time roaming the field, and women found him desirable.

He had the high optimism so characteristic of the sons and daughters of immigrants. Their parents remembered their hopeless poverty in the land they had left to come to America and often told their children about their poverty—how they had crossed the sea in steerage, seeking a new life. They had left the Old World seeking riches and freedom in the New. They had come hoping for freedom to worship as they saw fit, to escape tyrannical governments, to a land where they and their children could walk with head erect and free from the scourge of poverty.

For this they crossed the sea. There were no Ramada Inns waiting for them when they arrived. On the contrary, there was poverty and anxiety; but there was also freedom, adventure and opportunity. There were no rigid caste lines; the spoils belonged to the strongest and the shrewdest. They took this forbidding continent, and with their brawn, with their labor, with their passionate belief in their destiny, they turned it into the greatest production and distribution machine the world has ever known.

They wanted passionately to be completely American, to learn the language, to succeed. For this they labored twelve hours a day, never dreaming that they were the forebears of generations that would see the highest standard of living in the world. America and its promises sang like a litany in the hearts of the oppressed throughout Europe and Asia. Intoxicated by the song of freedom and the melody of hope and fortune, they poured into the United States, whose doors were thrown open for them in a historic embrace of welcome unparalleled in recorded history. They came —Polish, Italian, Irish, German, Swedish, English, Hungarian, Catholic, Protestant, Jew—all animated by the same needs and hungers and hopes.

The malcontents, the dreamers of dreams came and spent their vigor and vitality on molding the nation into strength and promise where dreams became realities. They labored, they toiled, they lived in crowded quarters. They were poor, they struggled to learn the language of their new land; and as they endured their poverty, they were heartened by their children's successes. They perceived that through their diligence and fortitude their children would be freed from the ignominy of poverty and ignorance. So the sunshine of hope was with them. They moved westward and cleared the land and saw golden wheat glisten in the rain and sun. They were conquerors, and they gave to their children an élan, a vitality, an optimism, an assurance that there was nothing they could not do.

Theirs was the will, and the earth was rich with growth, and in the womb of the earth was oil and coal. But more than physical resources was the heritage they brought with them: the creativity of the Italians, the Irish spirit of rebellion, the German thoroughness, the British discipline, the Catholic morals, the innovativeness of the Protestant, the ever present intellectuality of the Jew. This land became a caldron of mixtures unknown at any other period in all of history.

Unique and startling, this amazing blend of heritages produced a people of strength and generosity. The gods gave all the gifts of mankind to this nation, and superbly this nation used them to produce a pattern of freedom, production and constant progress.

The second generation, the inheritors of these gifts, became the conquerors. They brought their success and their worldly goods to their parents—it was their accolade. The older generation was not banished to a tragic and sad estate as in our contemporary life-style in which a man at sixty years of age becomes a non-person—useless and unwanted. To the contrary, they were revered and treated with tenderness.

Francesconio, like most all of the second generation —the sons and daughters of the immigrants—entertained a deep love and regard for his parents and shared his success with them. He was a happy man, adjusted to his life-style and the time in which he lived. He had no psychological shadows, no inferiority complexes. He never worried who he was. He was a big man, with a great laugh.

He enjoyed women and was Italian enough to enjoy beauty in any form, particularly women. He had seen the picture of Molly in the paper and was struck with her beauty.

One of his friends who frequently took Cynthia Parker out for dinner said to him, "You should see her in living color; then you will know how beautiful she really is."

So a dinner was arranged, and Francesconio met Molly and fell madly and deeply in love with her. But three times married with nine children and of the Jewish faith! Francesconio knew the arguments against such a marriage, but what did they count for compared to Molly's beauty and her captivating honesty.

Molly told her sister, Bertha, and me (Molly's niece, Bertha's daughter) about the Italian and how good-looking he was.

"Look," she told my mother, "he gave me this ring."

"So," said my practical mother, "he gave you a ring. How many rings do you need? You have three engagement and three wedding rings, so you need another ring on your fingers!"

"Bertha, I only wear the engagement rings, not the wedding bands, because I'm not married anymore."

"*Nu* if you don't wear the wedding rings because Sol, Al and Bill are dead—may their souls rest in peace —why do you wear the engagement rings they gave you?"

Molly shrugged. "They didn't die when we were engaged, only after we were married."

"*Nu*, so what?" said her sister. (My mother began almost every sentence with *nu*, which means "so, indeed, you don't say." It is difficult to define, but it adds an exclamation to a statement, and Aunt Molly always affected my mother so that she became exasperated, perplexed and dumbfounded.)

"What has that got to do with the fact that they died after you were married?"

Triumphantly, Molly retorted, "That's the point! When I wear the engagement rings, I don't have to think about their dying."

"All right," said my mother, "but if a man gives a woman a ring, that means only one thing—an engagement."

"You are too old-fashioned," said Molly. "It just means he likes to give rings."

"So he likes to give rings. If he met me, would he give me a ring?"

"So why not?" said Aunt Molly.

"Should I take a ring from a Gentile and a Catholic?" retorted my mother. "A Baptist was bad enough and an Episcopalian but now a Catholic! Your grandfather, blessed be his memory, if he were alive would tear his hair."

I couldn't help laughing, "Mama. How could Grandpa tear his hair? He didn't have any."

"All right, all right," said my exasperated mother, "so he wouldn't tear his hair. Give your Italian friend back his ring and tell him you are not going to marry a Catholic."

"Who says I'm going to marry him? There will be no wedding," said Molly.

"*Nu*, so give it back to him, and tell him you can't take a ring from him because you are not going to marry a Catholic."

Molly answered, "I'm not giving back the ring. I'll keep this one, and I want an engagement ring too."

"You are *meshugge*! You are not going to marry him, but you want an engagement ring! What are you going to do—open a jewelry store? What kind of a *mishegoss* is this?"

"I want the engagement ring because I'm going to

live with him, but I won't marry him, because if I do he will die."

This left my mother speechless. "Maybe I should tear my hair now! What are you saying to me that you will live with a Catholic but won't marry him? Is this the kind of religion Catholics believe in? He wants to take a nice Jewish widow to live with him? Well, what do you expect from a Catholic? What kind of a man is he? And you want to take an engagement ring from him? It's a disgrace! You want the family to be disgraced, too?"

"Don't get excited. He wants to marry me; I won't marry him."

My mother was stunned into an agonized silence. "What—what did you say?"

"I said," said Molly, "that I won't marry him. I told you when Sol died that I would never marry again, but I want to live with Francesconio."

My mother figuratively tore her hair. "What do you mean you won't ever marry again?"

"Because if I do and he becomes my husband, he will surely die."

"But, Aunt Molly," I protested, "everybody dies ultimately."

"But not everyone dies immediately after marrying as my three husbands died. You want I should be a widow again?"

"But, Molly, that's crazy!"

Aunt Molly looked reproachfully at me, "So, my sister tells me I'm *meshugge*, and my niece says I'm crazy. You just show me any other woman who has buried three husbands in five years. Show me one! Just one!"

My mother, appalled at Aunt Molly's intentions,

found herself abandoning her objections to marriage to a Catholic. Suddenly she began arguing in favor of such a marriage. "You are going to live in sin here in the city where people know you? You are going to send out wedding announcements saying Mrs. Davidson announces that she will live with whatever his name is though she is not married to him. Is that what you are going to do?"

"Well," said Molly, "I'm not going to put a sign out on the house, but I'm not going to marry Francesconio."

"So give him up."

"But I love him."

"Love," snorted my mother, "love is a *mishegoss*. You marry so you can have children and a man to support you."

"I know, I know," said Aunt Molly, "but you should see Francesconio. He is good to look at."

"Molly, I'm not interested in his looks. All right, he's a Catholic, but at least marry him. It's bad enough to have another Gentile and a Catholic, but to live with him—what kind of woman does that? Why don't you marry Abe Goldstein? He's a nice-looking boy, and in two years he'll be a doctor."

Molly looked astonished. "Why should I marry the Goldstein boy?"

Mother was so upset that she shouted at Aunt Molly, "Because he's a good Jewish boy who will take care of his family, and I can tell by the way he looks at you that he would marry you!"

"Let him look. I won't marry him. He looks like a fish to me."

"A fish? Why a fish?"

"Because everyone looks like some kind of animal."

"So what do you look like?" Mama demanded.

"Aunt Molly can resemble only one animal—a bird of Paradise," I said.

This was too much for my mother. Now she turned to me in anger. "My own daughter thinks I look like an animal!"

"Mama, what nonsense! If Aunt Molly thinks everyone looks like an animal, she must resemble one, also."

My mother said scornfully, "And so what kind of animal do I look like?"

She wouldn't let me answer but went on with her diatribe. "So my own flesh and blood thinks her mother resembles an animal!" And with that she began chopping the herring that she was preparing for a salad. No herring was ever pounded so angrily.

Molly rose to leave. "You'll see," she said. "You will like Francesconio."

"Molly, listen to me. If you will at least marry him, I'll promise to like him even if he is a *goy*."

Aunt Molly gathered up her skirts, daubed her nose with a bit of powder with a lace-edged perfumed handkerchief and left, saying, "Remember, Bertha, I'm not getting married."

11

So Molly went home wearing another diamond ring with an enormous stone. In the streetcar she kept gazing at the stone with delight and looked forward to showing it to Cynthia and to Alice, but first she must talk to the boys.

She hoped she wouldn't have any trouble, but Molly was an optimist by nature and was sure the boys would be as happy as she was. She noticed as she walked up the steps that the yard was spic-and-span. Michael had taken care of it. It really was Robert's week to do the yard, but a trade-in marble had freed Robert to do what he wanted and had added to Michael's collection of marbles.

It was six-thirty, and the boys would all be home. It was time for supper. Mrs. Kolensky prepared the dinner and set the table, but the boys would do the supper dishes. They took turns—two of them evey night. Molly smiled to herself—they were good children. But as she entered the house she heard raised voices. An argument was going on. All the boys except Jonas were in the living room; he was in the basement, carving. It was his passion, and Molly was sure he was going to be a great sculptor someday.

Michael cried, "Aunt Molly!" and the boys came

up and kissed her. It was one of Molly's rules. The boys kissed her when she came home and in the morning when they left for school.

"Why all the kissing?" asked her sister, Bertha. "Is it a wedding every time you come home? What foolishness is it this kissing."

But Molly was adamant. She wanted the nine boys to feel that she loved them, and she wanted them to love her. Besides, it gave them a sense of belonging—an emotional security, and while Molly was not a trained psychologist, she intuitively felt their need for emotional security.

"So what's the argument about?"

Robert, aged thirteen, had been seen walking home with a girl, carrying her books. The rest of them were quizzing him. Robert had red hair and a quick temper.

"I'll walk home with whom I want, and it's none of your business. If you want to know, I'm going into business with her."

Irwin hooted. "What kind of business?"

"Well, it's none of your business, so you can all shut up!"

Aunt Molly sat down. "Listen, if Robert wants to walk home with a girl, what's wrong with that? I'm glad you carried her books for her—that's nice. Donald, why are you scratching yourself?"

"I don't know. I guess 'cause it itches."

"Well, stop it," said Aunt Molly, "because I want to talk to all of you. Call Jonas and tell him to come upstairs. It's time for supper, but before we sit down I want to tell all of you something."

"Gosh, Aunt Molly, I'm hungry. Can't we eat first?"

"No, all of you sit down."

There were three couches so that the nine boys would have room to sit in the living room, Molly had explained while furnishing the house.

"Sit down, all of you. First, I want you to see my diamond. It's from Francesconio. I'm going to live with him like his wife." But she would not go through a ceremony, and she explained her reasons. Also, she told them that she wouldn't make any arrangements unless they approved of Francesconio.

"Now," said Molly, "I'm going to leave you so you can discuss Francesconio and tell me how you feel about his coming to live here."

Since they had already met him, the discussion was lively. Michael objected. "Why should she bring him here to live? She's not lonely. She's got all of us, and where are we going to put him? All the bedrooms are filled."

"Don't be such a creep," said Irwin. "He will sleep in Aunt Molly's room."

Michael was obdurate. "Why do we need a stranger? What can he do for Aunt Molly that we can't?"

"Well, for one thing he's rich and can give Molly anything she wants."

"Well, I don't want him, and I vote against him. Besides, he chucked me under my chin and I hate chuckers."

"Chuckers? Where did you acquire that word, may I ask?"

"Oh, he makes up all sorts of words," volunteered Jonas. "He thinks he's a genius."

"I don't think so. I know so. I wish you'd get facts right," retorted Michael.

Donald, who was very quiet and spent most of his

time practicing football, spoke up. "I don't like his hair."

"What's the matter with his hair?"

"Nothing. I just don't like the way he wears it. Why doesn't he part his hair?"

"You're nuts," Irwin told him. "What's that got to do with his living here?"

"Nothing. I just thought you ought to know I don't like the way he combs it."

"What about you, Douglas?"

"I like him, but I don't want him living here. He takes enough of Molly's time now. What will it be like if he lives here? Anyhow, he reminds me of my uncle, and I hate him."

"Who—him or your uncle?"

"My uncle, you creep."

"Ya, I know, but why do you hate your uncle? He always brings Aunt Molly a bottle of wine when he comes."

"What good is that? Aunt Molly nor any of us drink it. Anyhow, he's got sweaty hands, and he always puts them on my shoulder and presses down on my bones. When he does that, if that's his idea of a hug, I wish he'd stay away."

Victor, who had been silent, now spoke up. "Hey, have you ever watched Francesconio?"

"What do you mean have I watched him? Why should I?"

"He looks like my dog."

"Like your dog, you're crazy!"

"I'm not crazy. You just watch him. He follows Aunt Molly around the house and keeps looking at her every minute just like my dog looks at me."

"Nuts! You and your dog."

Jonas, who was finicky about food, worried Aunt Molly because he didn't eat enough. He now spoke up, "He's Italian and I hate spaghetti, and if he lives here we will have spaghetti morning, noon and night."

"Gee," broke in Michael, "it could be worse. He could be Chinese, and then we'd have Chinese food. If she has to bring someone else into the house, why doesn't she choose a guy that makes candy?"

"So far," Irwin said sarcastically, "I have one I don't like his hair; one He looks like a dog; one He is a chucker of chins; one that he'll take up too much room in the house; one that he's Italian. So, how do we vote? Five against him? That means we don't want Francesconio?"

"Who is going to tell Aunt Molly?"

"You tell her, Kenneth. You're the oldest."

"But what do I tell her? That you don't like the way he parts his hair? What kind of a reason is that?"

"Sure, just tell her the truth."

"All right, I'll do it. But what happens if Aunt Molly starts to cry?" asked Jonas.

"Well, what happens when you cry?"

"I don't cry. I'm not a crybaby."

"Well, maybe you don't cry; but I hate that feeling in my throat when I cry. It would be awful if Aunt Molly would cry. I couldn't stand it. I'd cry in sympathy."

Irwin's twin, Isadore, who was as precise and prudent as though he were thirty years old instead of thirteen and a half, said, "Well, it's Aunt Molly's house, and if she wants to bring some guy in here even if we don't like his hairdo—and I hate his hairdo, too, —and whenever you turn around he's here. The house

88

won't be like it's always been, because he'll be every-where in this house. He will fill the house, but if Aunt Molly wants him, what can we do about it?"

"I like the way he dresses," Douglas said, who was the neatest of all the boys.

"It's too late. We've got five votes against him."

"They are all silly reasons. When people vote for a president or a senator, it's not on how they part their hair or whether he's an Italian. They vote for him whether he's a Democrat or Republican."

"Oh, shut up, Michael. We don't know whether he's a Republican or a Democrat, and he isn't running for office."

"Yes he is," Michael insisted. "He's running for the office of husband for Aunt Molly, and that's what we are voting for." Now Michael was really roused. "Do we really want an Italian in the house? Do you know what the Romans did to the Carthaginians? They de-stroyed the whole city."

"What the dickens do the Carthaginians or whatever you call them have to do with Francesconio?"

"He inherits their blood. Do we want a guy like that in our house?"

"What's so wonderful about you?" asked Irwin. "Look what the English did to poor Mary Queen of Scots. They chopped off her head."

"Am I responsible for the English? I'm not English, I'm Irish. I hate the English."

"You hate too many people."

"Well, I've got a big hater in me. I can hate a lot more people than you can."

"Oh, shut up, all of you! What are we going to tell Aunt Molly?"

"Nothing but the truth," said Isadore. "That's what

Aunt Molly always insists we do. So let's tell her the truth that we don't like Francesconio, but if she marries him, we will be polite to him, but that's all. He is a stranger, and he's barging in on us."

"Ya, and he keeps her up so late, she'll be tired out," piped up Kenneth.

So the boys assured Aunt Molly that if that's what she wanted and was going to bring Francesconio into the house, they would be polite to him, but that was all, because he was an outsider.

Molly kissed them and thanked them and assured them that when they knew him better they would be keen about him.

And then she said, "Let's have him to dinner!"

12

That night my mother told my father Molly's decision. *"Vay iz mir"* ("Woe is me"), said my mother, lapsing into Yiddish. "What kind of craziness is this, I ask you? My father, blessed be his memory, would rise from his grave. The whole family will be disgraced. She is crazy, my sister. In the whole city, in the whole country, only my sister talks to God."

"Now, Bertha, she didn't say she talks to God; she said she knows that God doesn't want her to get married again," said my father.

"She knows God's intentions," snorted my mother. "Tell me, in all Talmudic writings, was there ever anything like this? Why should this curse fall on me?"

"But, Mama," I said, "you must admit that there was something strange about Molly's three husbands dying so quickly after their marriage. Besides, it's her own life."

"It's not her own life. If God speaks to her, He can speak to me too and tell me not to let my sister act crazy."

Papa, who never interfered in anything and was as mild a man as anyone could meet, protested. "Please, Bertha, it's enough that Molly thinks she knows what God is planning; don't you become an interpreter of

God's intentions as well. I've had a hard day. The grocery store was full of complainers today. Their bills weren't right or the corned beef was too dry, and I hear that Morris Solomon is opening a dairy store in the next block. I've got troubles of my own."

"But such a trouble, Ben. My worst enemy shouldn't have it."

Ben shrugged. My father was a very quiet man whose yearning was for learning and the ability to speak. Whenever there was a speaker scheduled, he used to go to lodge meetings; it was his only recreation. Sometimes he would steal away from his store to go to court to hear a famous lawyer argue a case. For my father good language, rolling sentences and eloquent phrases were like music.

One time he took me with him to hear a famous lawyer plead his case. "The power of words," he told me, "is greater than guns or cannon. Learn to use them. See what Lincoln did with a few words, and consider the Bible," he told me. "The words in the Bible have influenced mankind more than any armies or generals."

He had emigrated to the U.S. when he was seventeen. For him it was not fame and fortune that lured him, but a woman older than himself whom he followed when she emigrated to America.

My mother was haunted by that fact. She just couldn't believe that circumstances had drifted him and the woman apart and that she played no part in my father's life and not much in his memory.

How astonished some of his customers would have been to know what he was thinking of as he ladled out a couple of herrings for a customer. My mother would argue with him: Not words but pennies count. She would tell him, "It's dollars that speak, not words." Who knows how many geniuses were buried in little stores, trying to make a living out of pennies and dimes? How many peddlers with packs on their backs, selling merchandise to farmers before there were Sears and Roebuck catalogues, could have been writers or doctors or teachers? It was their vitality, their endurance, their ambition, that thrust this land into production and wealth. It was my father who gave me his dreams for beauty and his passion for freedom.

There were thousands like him grubbing away at making a living, enduring long hours, poverty, exclusion from the circles of the rich but sustained because they knew that opportunity was theirs. They were optimistic. It was the land of the free, and that meant the gates to achievement were open for all.

I loved my father for his tenderness and his dreams. One of them was fulfilled when he came home one night and announced to my mother that they had enough money saved for a down payment on a house. My mother sat down and cried. It was one of the few times I saw her demonstrative as she took my father's hand and held it tightly. I observed that both hands were toil-worn. The house they would buy was theirs by the right of their labor, and I made up my mind that someday I would make it possible for them to stop working so hard. But in that moment they had eyes and voice only for each other. It was their own personal dream come true.

And this night my father was particularly tired, and he wanted to stop my mother from arguing about Molly. Molly was a problem, and there was nothing he could do about it.

"Listen, Bertha, if God didn't want Molly to have so many husbands, He shouldn't have made her so *shayn* [beautiful]."

Now my mother, who could be unreasonable, suddenly looked at my father suspiciously. "So you think Molly is beautiful, and that's why you stick up for her instead of supporting your wife."

My father said wearily, "Look, Bertha, I've got my own troubles. Let Molly do what she wants—she will anyway."

But if my Aunt Molly was stubborn, so was my mother. The next day she washed her hair and asked me to do her nails and dressed in her best suit and hat. She was going to call on Francesconio.

"Mama, Aunt Molly will be angry when she finds out you went to see Francesconio," I said.

"Let her be mad. Would I stay quiet if I knew she was eating poison? What kind of a sister would I be?"

"But Mama, Aunt Molly knows what she wants to do, even if she is years younger than you."

"Never mind. He's a no-good, and he's just fooling around with her. Someone should tell him that he's a good-for-nothing *shaygets*."

The "good-for-nothing *shaygets*" had at that moment just negotiated a commission that would bring him some thousands of dollars' profit. When he was told that a Mrs. Fine wanted to see him, he presumed it was about some property. He was therefore caught off guard when she announced that she was Bertha Fine, the older sister of Molly Davidson.

He noted that she, too, was a handsome woman— though not, of course, the beauty that Aunt Molly was.

"I won't beat around the bush," she told him. "I want to ask you to stay away from my sister."

"Why?" asked the startled Francesconio. "What do you have against me?"

"I don't know you, so I don't know whether I have anything personal against you, but you are a Catholic, which isn't too bad because we know some nice Catholics. They buy their groceries from my husband. But Molly will never become a Catholic."

"I never asked her to change her religion," expostulated the surprised Francesconio. "That never came up."

"I know," said my mother, "but because she won't be converted, you are only too glad to accept her decision not to get married but to live with you. And that's why I've come here to ask you not to live with her. It will disgrace us, and your priest will disapprove. Can't you just move away and start your business in some other city?"

Francesconio didn't know whether to laugh or be angry. "No, I can't and won't move away. This is where I make my living, and for your information, Mrs. Fine, I make a good living and I can take care of your sister very well. And I do not want to live with her. I want to marry her. It's not my idea to live together without a marriage. You may not like my religion, but we believe in marriage, and I want to marry Molly. She's the one who is afraid to marry me, because she thinks I'll get sick or have an accident and die."

Bertha stared at Francesconio. Suddenly she saw a way out of this dilemma. They could be allies, she and Francesconio.

"You really don't want to live with her?"

"No, I don't. I told you I want to marry her."

"To tell you the truth," my mother confided, "I

don't want Molly to marry a Catholic. It won't work out. Catholics are against Jews, and Jews aren't in love with Catholics either, but rather than have Molly living with you unmarried, I'd not object to her marrying you."

Francesconio wondered what his mother would say if she heard Mrs. Fine say that the only reason she wouldn't object to the marriage was that it represented a lesser evil.

"Well, Mrs. Fine," he said, "what do you suggest I do?"

"Give Molly up. A nice man like you (suddenly he had become attractive in her eyes) can find a Catholic girl and be happy with her. You can have a church wedding, and your mother—may she live in peace— with such a nice son would have a daughter-in-law, and you could have some fine children, God willing."

Francesconio understood my mother's worry. He himself was appalled by Molly's notion, but he loved her—and secretly he admired her, too. She was a pretty wonderful human being to have taken nine boys into her home, and, God, was she beautiful. But what would the priest say. After all, he wasn't needed for the most part, only for weddings, funerals, and baptisms— they were the priests' domain. Not that Francesconio thought too seriously about the church, but there was a place for it, and certainly the business of marriage was the business of the church. And Molly's notion was crazy, as though getting married to her meant that he must die. Besides, if she loved him, she would give up this nonsense. On the other hand, he was fair enough to understand that from her point of view if he loved her enough he would live with her without marriage. But her notions were damn right ridiculous, and if he gave in to this nonsense of not marrying her, he would be the laughing stock of his friends. Molly must be persuaded that her notion had no validity, and that was his job. And he was sure he could persuade her—but, then, he didn't know Molly's determination very well.

13

That night my mother triumphantly reported to my father and me that she had told Francesconio what she thought of Molly's craziness and she added, when she was through, maybe he too thought telling him about Molly was a little crazy.

I was appalled. "Mama, how could you do such a thing to Molly? You know she isn't crazy."

"So maybe I went a little far, but you want for me to let my sister disgrace us all?"

"Well, I don't see how you've helped matters, because if Molly feels that way about Francesconio, she'll never get married. So what have you accomplished?"

"Beets should grow in my stomach [a popular Jewish saying] if I should let Molly make a fool of herself. So I went to see his mother."

"Whose mother?"

"Francesconio's mother. A nice Italian lady. I gave her my recipe for making chicken soup."

"Chicken soup? What has that got to do with Mrs. Valedara? She wasn't sick."

"So what did you think I would go empty-handed? I brought her some chicken soup and she tasted it, and *Gott sei dank* (thank God), she liked it. So I told her how to make it, and she said she would, and that she would give some to the priest."

"Why to the priest?"

"He has a weak stomach, and I told her it would be good for him."

My father interrupted. "Did you go to see Mrs. Valedara to help her priest's stomach?"

My mother gave my father a pitying glance. "So I should break right in with a conversation about her son? In society you first talk about everything but not for the real reason I came."

"Who told you about society, Bertha? Remember, I'm just a storekeeper."

"So, my *hertzel* (my heart), good enough you are for anyone, but Mrs. Valedara lives in a big house, and a *schvartze* opened the door for me. That's pretty good society. So we sat down and I told her what a nice boy her son was and that he was a real *mensh* (fine human being) and that he was sad about losing Molly, but was it right, I asked her, for a man to live with a woman to whom he isn't married? No, she didn't think that was right, and she wondered about the Jewish religion. She didn't know they lived together without a wedding, though she knew their religion was different from hers.

"What did you say to that?"

"What did I say? I told her all about our bar mitzvahs, just like their communion, and how we get married, that our Bible tells us God said we should be fruitful and multiply, just like their religion, and that's why Molly's family was against her ideas and how she should tell her son it's wrong to live like Molly wants."

"But didn't you tell her about Molly's marriages that ended so quickly, so at least she understood why Molly feels that way?"

"Yes, yes. I told her."

"What did she say?"

"Say? She shook her head and said, 'I wanna tell my boy.' "

"But her boy knows all about it, so what good will your visit do?" I asked.

"You think maybe your mother isn't so smart? Maybe not with books but with people, yes."

After this modest approval of herself, my mother rose to make herself some tea.

"How did you get downtown to Francesconio's office?"

"I took the streetcar. Three of them."

"How did you know where his mother lives?"

"How did I know? I asked him."

"Did he know that you wanted to talk to his mother about Molly? He must have thought that you were a busybody."

"By the time I was through with him, his *kop* was *ferdreht* [his head was in a turmoil]."

What we did not know then but later understood was that Molly had a neurosis, a complex, a sense of insecurity and a sense of guilt that caused her to refuse to marry anyone. Somehow she felt that she was responsible for the deaths of her three husbands. Bill fell down the elevator shaft because she was waiting for him to bring her a blouse from the factory. If she hadn't told him to hurry, Bill would have looked where he was going.

When Al, her second husband, fell from the roof he was repairing, it was also because he was hurrying to finish the job so he could rush home because she was waiting for him to go to a friend's house for supper.

When Sol, her third husband, assured her that he

would be better in a few days, she should, she felt, have paid no attention to his assurances and called in a specialist, who might have saved Sol.

If a Freud or a Jung were analyzing her, or any of the many different schools of psychiatry, they would surely have discovered her neurosis, and perhaps telling about the experiences might have freed her from this complex. But so deep-rooted was her fear that another husband would die that her defense was to deny the act of marriage itself, and thus she would be safe from another devastating experience. All the talking in the world could not move Molly. The neurosis was too powerful.

Francesconio was shaken by my mother's visit, and his own mother wept and carried on that it was bad enough that Molly wasn't a Catholic, but to live in sin—and what would the children be? Of course she wanted him to be happy, but look at all the beautiful Italian girls, and she began to name them.

"Yes, yes. I know, I know, but I don't want any of them. I want Molly Davidson."

Like mothers throughout the ages, her one panacea was eating, and without realizing the irony of it, Mrs. Valedara told Francesconio that she had some delicious chicken soup that Molly's sister had brought her.

"I don't want that meddling woman's soup. What business did she have to come here and tell you the story?"

But the fact was that Francesconio was troubled. Molly's idea was wild and he disapproved of it; he was not, he decided, going to be made a laughingstock among his friends. What kind of marriage would that be?

So he met Molly and told her that unless she was

willing to marry him the whole thing was off. He wasn't going to see her anymore.

He loved her. He wanted her for his own. He wanted to make love to her. He wanted to go to bed with her. He wanted to see her in his arms. He wanted to look at her lovely face lying in his arms. What did she think he was made of, stone? Had she forgotten that he was Italian and a man of great passion?

Molly said she hadn't forgotten that he was Italian and that he had passion. No, Molly told him, she was aware of all these things, and did he think she had no passion? That she didn't want to belong to him? She'd have him know, she said, that when he touched her, she had shivers all through her body. So why didn't he be reasonable and just live with her?

Maybe she could get the nice Goldstein boy, he told her, to acquiesce to such an agreement, but he was a man and he wanted a wife.

"But I will be a wife except I don't want a marriage ceremony." And as for the Goldstein boy, if that was what Francesconio wanted, she would give him back his ring and marry the Goldstein boy, "who, if you please," she said, "will soon be a doctor."

"What do you mean you would marry him? If you would marry him, why won't you marry me?"

"It's very simple," said Molly. "I don't love him, so I wouldn't care if he died, but for you I feel differently."

So there they stood, staring at each other. Molly in tears, and Francesconio as near to tears as he had been in years. Molly rose from her chair and dropped to her knees and put her arms around Francesconio.

"I love you. I love you. Don't give me up. Take me,

cherish me, for if you go away tonight, I don't want to see you anymore for my heart hurts. Here, Francesconio, here," and Molly placed his hand on her heart. "It hurts and I don't know what to do. To marry you and every day to be tortured that something is going to happen to you. I can't take it. I'd rather give you up now."

Francesconio was torn between tenderness and sympathy for Molly and his disbelief that Molly would allow an absurd notion to stand between them.

"I'm leaving you now, Molly. If you really loved me, you would marry me. By your refusal I'm convinced you really don't care. If you change your mind, let me know, because while I love you, I am not going to allow you to make a fool of me." With that Francesconio, torn now between anguish and anger, took up his hat and left.

Molly was in despair, but then her pride came to her rescue. If he didn't believe her, let him go. But that, she found, was easy to say, and as the days went by, her pain was no less. Her one hope was that Francesconio would come back. And he was saying similar things to himself. And as the days continued to pass, Molly, frozen by her fear, made no move, and Francesconio, believing that Molly's attitude was irrational, made no move either.

Both were suffering from what appeared to be irreconcilable differences.

14

It was June 1914. The lights of Europe were about to go out—as Lord Grey was to say a little later. The Austrians had danced to the Strauss waltzes and had given the world a joyous hour. But the world was soon to dance to another tune—an elegy of death and destruction.

In Vienna, Franz Josef, Emperor of Austria-Hungary, sat with bowed head, a figure of tragedy. His brother, Maximilian, denied a kingdom in Europe, had listened to the siren song of the exiled Mexicans and crossed the ocean to become their emperor. But before he left, Franz Josef demanded that Maximilian officially renounce any rights to the Austrian-Hungarian empire; a renunciation that proved to be superfluous, for his kingdom in Mexico ended for him before a firing squad.

The emperor's son, Rudolph, committed suicide, and Franz Josef cried bitterly, "He died like a tailor."

His wife, Elizabeth, was stabbed as she stepped on a boat returning to Vienna. The emperor kept the pillow on which her head rested as she died in a frame above his head.

His sister died in a fire. He was surrounded by

tragedy, and if he could have foreseen the future, he would have heard the drums of doom for his empire.

Franz Ferdinand, a nephew who was heir to the throne, had married beneath himself. She was only a countess, and because of that she was treated shabbily at court. To compensate, Franz Ferdinand went visiting the Serbs, who always made a fuss over the countess. But at Sarajevo he and his countess were assassinated as they drove through the streets in an automobile.

Immediately the Austrian military group urged the Emperor to invade Bosnia and teach them a lesson. But the Emperor was old, eighty-four; he wanted no war; he knew the cosmic price of a general war and resisted the militarists, who wanted to march into Bosnia at once. The military group overwhelmed him with their enthusiasm for war which he resisted. But fate decreed otherwise, for in Berlin, Kaiser Wilhelm II of Germany was not only dedicated to military activities but made a point of always maintaining a military bearing. He had a personal reason for his passion for everything that pertained to war and battles. Because he was born with a withered arm his life was devoted to proving that he was vigorous and able in spite of this congenital handicap. He rode a horse magnificently, having overcome the imbalance caused by the withered arm.

His cousin George, King of England, he was determined should never feel that he was a better man than he Wilhelm. The assassination at Sarajevo was his opportunity. This was to be his hour. The countess and Franz Ferdinand's deaths would allow him to play the hero's part.

A treaty between Austria-Hungary and Germany

for mutual aid gave the Kaiser his excuse, and before the Emperor could object, the Kaiser exultantly cried "To arms!" and a generation was doomed because the Kaiser behaved as though he were a medieval knight and not a modern ruler. Had he but known it, he was doomed to defeat and to live unsung and unloved and uncrowned.

For the two Austrians who were practically unknown —Countess Sophie and Franz Ferdinand the heir apparent to the Austrian-Hungarian throne—Flanders Field would bloom with the red poppies of death. The United States was to be hurled from her safe position urged 155 years earlier by George Washington of no embroilments, into two wars and into the responsibility of bearing the financial burden of all the nations devastated by the war.

In that year Irwin and his twin, Isadore, were eighteen years old. It was also the year they were graduated from high school. For the commencement exercises the whole tribe was in attendance—all the boys, Aunt Molly, Bertha and her husband, Mrs. Kolensky and me.

It was a great day for Molly. For four years the boys had been her responsibility, and this night two of them were in the graduating class. It was a victory for her.

Before the whole procession left the house, Molly spoke to Irwin and Isadore: "For your father I would wish he should see this night. I want you should talk to all your brothers. They should be like you and go to school, and I should have more nights like this night. And now we have a surprise for you. Victor, you come and give your brothers our present."

So Victor, who was the only soft-spoken one of the nine, came forward and handed Irwin and Isadore each a package. He had written a speech but was now tongue-tied, and when he stepped forward to give the twins their present he merely said, "Here it is."

Molly had supplied most of the money but had insisted that the card read "from Aunt Molly and all of us." It was part of Molly's magic to make the nine boys feel they belonged together.

So Irwin and Isadore each had a watch to put in his pocket, and even when the war proved that wristwatches were not worn only by sissies (which was the first reaction to the wristwatch when it appeared in the country; it was the men in uniform who started using wristwatches, because it was easier than trying to pull a watch out of a pocket, particularly in the trenches), each continued to carry his watch.

As Molly sat in the audience, she remembered their father and said to Bertha, "I wish Sol—may he rest in peace—could see his boys get their diplomas." As each of the boys received his diploma through the years, Molly had it framed and hung in the dining room. For the dining room with the hung diplomas and the vacant spots for the diplomas which were still to be filled was a memory that comforted and challenged them.

Michael, sitting next to Molly in the auditorium, whispered, "Geez, Aunt Molly, I'll never get old enough to get a diploma and a watch. The world will end before I do."

Douglas, sitting in front, overheard Michael. "Where did you get your information that the world will end? Did the President of the United States tell you that in order to prevent your graduation? God is going to destroy the world? You know what? You're nuts!"

"All right, you'll see. I'll never make it."

Mrs. Kolensky shushed both of them. The class was

beginning its march down the aisle to the platform.

Aunt Molly's hat with its ostrich plumes moved gallantly as she turned her head to watch Irwin and Isadore. Both boys were dark-eyed with coal black hair. Irwin was outgoing and casual; Isadore was far more self-contained. The question in Molly's mind was should she send them to a Catholic college. After all, they were Sol's sons and they were Jewish. Marquette was a Catholic college, and Bertha had objected and pointed that out to Aunt Molly.

"So," said Aunt Molly, "where is there a Jewish college? And I'm not sending them to a college to get more Jewish. They are Jewish enough. Didn't I send them to Sunday school? What I want for Irwin is to be a lawyer, and Isadore, a doctor; and Marquette is cheaper than other colleges. It's right here in Milwaukee, so they can live at home, and I want for them to stay home. They can help me with the other boys."

"In the first place," I interrupted, "Isadore doesn't want to be a doctor. He told me he wants to be a teacher."

Aunt Molly was disturbed. "A nice Jewish boy should be a lawyer or a doctor."

"He can be a nice Jewish boy and not be a doctor," spoke up my father, who was listening to the conversation. "Let one of the Baptist boys be a doctor."

"A Baptist should be a doctor!" exclaimed Bertha with horror.

"Yes, why not? If some Baptists didn't become doctors, there just wouldn't be enough doctors to take care of everyone."

"You think the other boys should go to the Catholic college, too?"

My father shrugged his shoulders. "Molly, maybe all the boys don't want to go to college."

Molly looked anxious. "I want for all of them to go."

"So what's the matter with Marquette?" my father continued. "You think I should worry if the iceman who brings me ice is Jewish or Episcopalian. Do I care if the fishman who sells me fish is a Baptist? It's a *mishegoss.* Bertha, this is America, not the old country. We live together." Now he was challenging Bertha.

"You think maybe I should tell the cigarman I buy cigars only from Jewish salesmen? And what about my customers? Mrs. Anderson is a nice old lady. Should I tell her no milk for her if she isn't Jewish? Isn't her five cents as good as a Jew's? Does she ask me if I'm Jewish? And what about Father Flanagan, who buys a whole salami every week? Should I say no salami because you are a Catholic?"

Now my father was really roused. "Do you think I left Russia to worry that everyone wasn't Jewish? I want for everyone to be my friend."

"But, Papa," I broke in, "you go to the Temple."

"That's different," said Ben. "When I pray, I pray like a Jew; but in my store I don't ask God to listen in. There I'm friends with everybody. In the Temple where I put on my prayer shawl, I should suddenly surprise God and not be a Jew?"

And then my father spoke in more serious tones than usual. "You should know, my daughter, that in the Temple I pray not for myself but for all the Jews, and I pray like my father and my father's father did throughout the years. I pray as they did, and I pray that the Ten Commandments will be upheld."

It was as though my father were renewing the old

covenant between God and the Jews that man must regulate his relationship with his fellow men according to his relationship with God.

Irwin and Isadore had listened to this tirade, and Irwin in the privacy of their bedroom later that evening said to Isadore, "Ben was pretty wrought up. I don't think I want to be such a fervent Jew. The Episcopalians don't get so excited by their religion."

"How do you know what the Episcopalians feel?" asked Isadore.

"Well, they sure aren't as nutty about being Jewish as some Jews are. You remember when our Rabbi and Episcopal minister came to call and the Baptist minister? They got along first-rate; being Jewish or Episcopalian didn't seem to make so much difference to them. Besides, what suddenly gives with Aunt Molly? She married a Baptist and an Episcopalian as well as one father who was Jewish."

"That's the point," Irwin said. "She thinks because our father was Jewish she has to send us to a Jewish college."

"Well, I don't care," said Isadore. "All this stuff about tradition and religion is for the birds."

"Why don't you believe in God?"

"What kind of dumb question is that?"

"That's not a dumb question. I once asked Aunt Molly that."

"What did she say?"

"She said sure she did, but she thought that maybe God was confused with all the different ways people believed in Him."

"God confused! Only Molly could personalize God in that fashion."

"Well, maybe she's got something. I think it's crazy to have so many different churches, and I don't think God likes Jews any better than he does Baptists."

"Her sister sure does. You know what she told Molly at our graduation?"

"What?"

"She said it was time for Molly to send back all the boys to their aunts and uncles and let them assume the responsibility and that she should get married."

"And I suppose to a nice Jewish well-to-do man. What did Molly answer?"

"Just what would you expect? 'Please, Bertha,' she protested. 'You want I should have beets in my stomach? I would worry so I couldn't enjoy being married. I would worry he would die.' 'A *mishegoss!*' Bertha snorted."

So Irwin and Isadore enrolled at Marquette University, where they achieved high averages and to Molly's pride and delight were on the Dean's List. They were known as the twins whose Aunt Molly was the most beautiful woman in town.

But 1914 stepped into 1915, and then it was 1916 and 1917, and America entered the war—pushed in by German atrocities. Then it was as though the floodgates of emotion were opened, for hundreds of thousands of young Americans besieged the recruiting offices to volunteer to fight for their country. Sons of immigrants poured out their love for their America, the land that had given sanctuary to their parents. They expressed their passionate gratitude, their pride in America; they would die for her though those who enlisted thought little of death. Their sense of adventure and their loyalty and their anger at the Kaiser animated them. It was their parents who shuddered and who saw no glory but only death in the war.

For Molly, the war was a terrible thing, but it did not affect her life. Besides, the boys were too young to be hurt by the war. But Molly was soon to discover that the war could not be kept from touching her life; it was all-engulfing; it was like a forest fire that consumed and destroyed. That in every generation a form of nationalism took over, and man became the enemy of man.

15

After dinner one evening in May of 1917, Isadore and Irwin said, "Aunt Molly, could we see you?"

"What do you mean, Can you see Aunt Molly? You're looking at her now. What's with you two? 'Can we see you, Aunt Molly,' " and Jonas, who was a great mimic, mimicked Isadore's voice: " 'Can we see you, Aunt Molly?'

"Ladies and gentlemen, we are now to have a performance. The distinguished Marquette students with not a flunk to their credit are about to perform a miracle. They are to do something unique. They are begging permission to be allowed to look at Aunt Molly."

"Shut up, will you?" said Isadore. "Go upstairs and do your homework."

"Nix on that. I don't have to do my homework. I've done it, and I'm quite at leisure to observe this phenomenon," retorted Jonas.

"Listen, Aunt Molly, Irwin and I want to talk to you about something important."

Aunt Molly said, "So what is so important that the boys can't hear you? So talk, I'm listening."

"Well, it's difficult to tell and we don't want you upset, but we've made up our minds and we've thought about it very carefully."

Isadore's voice was trembling as it always did when he was very agitated.

"So tell already," said Aunt Molly. "Did you get in trouble at school?"

"Aunt Molly, how could Isadore get in trouble with his high grades? Maybe he's got a new girl. Maybe her parents object. Maybe she's turned him down."

"Will you shut up—all of you. The point is, Aunt Molly, Irwin and I are going to enlist."

"Enlist in what?" asked Aunt Molly, baffled by their agitation.

"In the army," said Irwin.

"In the army? What craziness is this? You are only nineteen years old. The whole U.S. is in the war, so the government needs you? You should stay home and finish school so your mother and father—may they rest in peace—should be proud of you."

There she goes, thought Irwin, *always bringing in our parents as though we were doing an injury to them.*

"Aunt Molly, it isn't a question of whether our parents would want us to enlist—it's a question of our duty."

"So who says it's your duty? Did the army ask you? Did they say to win the war, Isadore and Irwin Davidson are needed?"

"Of course not, Aunt Molly, but if everyone said it wasn't their job, who would defend our country?"

Molly was aghast. "Two nice boys like you! Are you going to defend your country with your fists? Nice boys don't touch guns, so what do you know about guns? You should please stay home and help me with the younger boys. You've never even touched a gun."

"We'll learn."

Mrs. Kolensky, who was standing at the kitchen door, put in her two cents' worth: "*Nu*, who will wash your socks and underwear, and where will you get a clean shirt every morning?"

Douglas broke in. "Does the U.S. Army know that you two don't eat bacon and eggs for breakfast but only oatmeal? You can't be a fighting soldier on oatmeal. I'm all for you being patriotic—as a matter of fact, Aunt Molly, if the war lasts a couple of more years, I'd like to join—but what good are Irwin and Isadore going to be in the army?"

Aunt Molly sank in her chair. "What have you got against the Germans? Is that why you want to fight?"

"Yes it is, Aunt Molly. It's the duty of every American. Germany sank our ships. Are we supposed to allow that, and have you forgotten what the Germans did to the Belgians?"

"Sure I remember, but grown-up Americans should enlist, not babies like you."

"Oh, come on, Aunt Molly. We're not babies, and you know it."

"What will your aunt and uncle say?"

"To tell you the truth, we don't care what they think. When we were younger, they weren't interested; they let you bear the responsibility of providing a home for us. We don't owe them anything. And, Aunt Molly, if anything happens to us, we'll leave our insurance to you so you can take care of the rest of the gang."

This was too much for Molly. "You see, already you talk of such things as dying. You want to break my heart?"

Before discussing the matter with Molly, Isadore and

Irwin had talked over what her reaction would be, "You know," said Irwin, "the first thing she'll say is that we will break her heart."

"I know and I guess we will. You know how soft-hearted she is. Aunt Molly's heart always breaks if anything goes wrong, but it always mends."

"What if she cries? That's going to be awful. I can't bear to see her do that."

"Well," said Irwin, "it's either watch her cry or give up enlisting. We will have to persuade her. We will know we've won if she says she hopes the Germans will have beets in their stomach. That's her favorite hate phrase."

So they had come prepared to face Molly, who now was really on the verge of tears.

"Aunt Molly, listen, do you want people to say that your boys aren't patriotic?"

"I want for people to say that Irwin and Isadore graduated with honors from Marquette University, that's what I want. I don't want to worry if your feet are wet or whether you've had enough to eat."

"Listen, Aunt Molly, when we come back we'll go back to Marquette and finish and get our degrees. We promise you."

"What if the war doesn't end for ten years like the Trojan War?" interjected Victor.

"Pipe down, will you," snapped Irwin. "Stay out of this."

"See," said Aunt Molly. "What will I do without you? How will I manage the boys?"

The truth was Molly was only thirty years old and more beautiful than ever. That she should have assumed the responsibility of taking care of nine boys was a heroic undertaking. Her whole family opposed it, but

Molly felt some inner compulsion to compensate for the fathers' deaths by keeping the boys together. If she could take care of them before their respective fathers died, she was resolved to assume the burden after their deaths, particularly when the insurance policies and the money were left to her. There was enough money to provide for their care and education. She never counted the psychic and emotional price she would have to pay, but then who in those days had heard about complexes and psychic energy? Aunt Molly did what her heart told her to do.

But Irwin and Isadore were determined to enlist in spite of Molly's tears and objections.

"Listen, Aunt Molly," said Isadore, "you say my father wouldn't rest in his grave if we go into the army. Irwin and I don't believe that. We think our father would approve. We think he would say it's only right that his sons should defend the U.S. Remember, our grandfather came to this country as an immigrant. The nation made him welcome. His son, our father, was born here, and it was his country, too; he would want us to support her in her hour of need. If he were alive he would enlist. Irwin and I think he would be proud of us—that's why we are going to enlist. Aunt Molly, there are thousands like us who feel the same way. We really never knew our mother—she was ill when we were little. You are the only mother we ever knew, and, Aunt Molly, we love you and we want you to be proud of us. Irwin and I promise you when we come back we'll never leave you."

There was silence in the room. Mrs. Kolensky was wiping her eyes, and Kenneth broke the silence by exclaiming, "Oh, gee wiz!" and ran out of the room and came back with the five-dollar gold piece his uncle had given him on his twelfth birthday. Kenneth was prepared to offer his priceless possession to Irwin and Isadore—until he realized that he didn't know how to divide it.

By this time Aunt Molly was in tears. "I am to lose both of you now when my heart hurts because I've lost Francesconio too. How can you do this to me and at such a time?"

That night Irwin and Isadore talked the matter over. Molly's distress and tears disturbed them. "What could we do about it?" asked Isadore.

"I've been thinking," said Irwin.

"O.K., O.K., so you've been thinking, but about what?"

"How to handle Aunt Molly."

"What do you mean handle her? That sounds crazy to me."

"I mean make it easier for her."

"You mean postpone our enlistment? I vote no to that. If we wait, the war could be over and we'd never get our chance."

"No, I'm not going to postpone my enlistment, either. I just think we ought to go and see Francesconio and find out if he still loves Aunt Molly, and if he does, ask him to live with her without a wedding."

"You mean we, you and I, should tell that to Francesconio? I wouldn't have the nerve. What if he doesn't love her anymore?"

"That's ridiculous. How could he not love Aunt Molly? She's the most beautiful woman in the whole city."

"Well, Aunt Molly herself told me she has seen him with other dates."

"When I broke up with Eileen, I used to take out Juanita just to make her jealous."

"Maybe you're right, but I don't think just because you dated two girls you are a specialist in love affairs. Besides, you are all wet, because you never did go back to Eileen."

"Well, if you want to know the truth, Eileen bores me and Juanita is a nothing. All she talks about is her skating."

"So what's all this heart-rending confession got to do with Aunt Molly and Francesconio?"

"I think we should take a gamble that he still loves her and see him and tell him that Molly really loves him but she's got this thing about not marrying anyone. Besides, can you think of anything else we can do?"

So the next day after classes Irwin and Isadore took the streetcar down to Francesconio's office. They decided not to phone for an appointment but to walk in unannounced. The young secretary had a special smile for the two earnest young men who asked to see Mr. Valedara.

"I'm sorry," she told them, "but Mr. Valedara is not in."

"Could we inquire when he will be in?"

"I don't really know. It depends on when the war ends because, you see, Mr. Valedara left yesterday for training—he enlisted for the duration of the war."

"Well, that's a fine kettle of fish. What do we do now?"

"Tell Aunt Molly the truth and tell her if Francesconio enlisted, it's right for us to do the same. We owe as much to our country as Francesconio does."

16

Francesconio was both clever and astute in his business. Each house he built brought him higher profits. He seemed to have a talent for buying land that became constantly valuable. Every time he built a house, he would sell it for a good profit, and with the profit he would buy more land. He was the first to build high-rise apartment buildings very close to Lake Michigan. Milwaukee Bay is frequently compared with the Bay of Naples in beauty. Through the years the land along the lake leading to Whitefish Bay became more and more valuable—beautiful homes graced the lake front, and Francesconio bought land and built and sold and became wealthier. Now he could afford to be generous. His charities began to be noticed— land for a parochial school, money to the hospital, money for the boys' club, etc.

As a bachelor, he was sought after and thoroughly enjoyed life. He had one of the first automobiles in Milwaukee and was becoming what was described as "a man about town." But he never lost his perspective. He never forgot his humble beginnings. His father had been a day laborer, but by the time Francesconio was a junior at high school, his father's arthritis prevented him from working, so Francesconio had to go to work.

He knew what it was like to be called a "dago" and to turn over to his mother every penny he made, so that there would be food in the house.

He was poor, but being poor was the accepted fate of most of the immigrants. They were looked down upon by the third- and fourth-generation Americans whose "superiority" rested upon the good fortune of having ancestors who had made the pilgrimage to the United States and struggled through austere times to attain success and fortune.

Francesconio made up his mind that no one was going to call him "dago." He had enough of that. The quickest way to achieve that, he believed, was to be successful; to make money. He was adventurous and was willing to work. Everybody worked. There was no leisure class in the United States. Anyone who did not work was scorned. Work and thrift produced the wealth needed for creating industries and building homes and roads and automobiles. It was the willingness to work that created the unparalleled productivity and wealth of the United States. The immigrants and their children were intoxicated with excitement and hope, for opportunity was open to everyone.

Francesconio was lucky too—an asset that some people seem to be born with, like violet-blue eyes or a quick laugh. The world is divided into the lucky and the unlucky. Francesconio took advantage of any luck that came his way. He had the courage to gamble that luck would stay with him. He knew, too, that he had not much education, so he absorbed all he could while listening to the older men in business and reading when he could.

He knew, also, that America was young and would

grow in population and in wealth and that land would be coveted and therefore increase in value. So with luck and astuteness, he began to build up a good-sized bank account.

When he met Molly he was devastated and thrilled by her beauty. Her lithesome figure reminded him of a flower bending to the wind. When the sun touched her hair, it made him think of shining gold and her eyes were pieces of the blue sky in a radiant day.

When he heard about the nine boys he was aghast. It was a crazy idea. Whoever heard of such a thing. A young woman assuming such a responsibility? Who would want to be entangled with such an involvement? Certainly not he—there were surely plenty of other beautiful women, but the truth was, he admitted to himself, he had never seen anyone as beautiful as Molly, and he began to admire her courage and the warm heart that made her feel responsible for the nine boys. They weren't a bad lot, and he was not going to allow them to stand between him and marrying Molly. The relatives of the boys should take care of them. It wasn't Molly's job. He was sure he could persuade her to give them up because she was in love with him as he was with her.

But he was to discover that it was not the boys that stood between them but that strange fixation of Molly's that she would never marry him but would live with him. Nothing would move her. She could not be per-suaded that he would not die if she married him.

He was convinced that if she really loved him she would give up that nonsensical idea of hers. He had stopped seeing Molly and dated other young women, but he could not put Molly out of his mind and heart.

But there was just too much between them—the boys, their own religious backgrounds, and then her refusal to marry him. Well, he was not going to be ridiculed by his friends. Besides, he was getting on in the business world and needed respectability. But argue as he did with himself, he could not shake his longing for Molly. The memory of her sweetness engulfed him every so often to such an extent that he found it difficult to keep from seeking her out.

His closest friend, with whom he frequently worked on certain projects, had announced to Francesconio that as soon as war was declared he was going to wind up his business affairs and enlist. Besides, he pointed out to Francesconio, the building business would probably come to a standstill until Germany was defeated. It never occurred to any Americans that there could be any other outcome of the war except defeat for Germany.

A few weeks later Francesconio, restless and unhappy about Molly, attended a bond rally. With a sudden decision, he put most of his cash in government bonds, made them out to his parents, in case he should be killed, and enlisted. He was sent as a candidate to officers' training school.

17

In 1908, Francesconio had enlisted in the National Guard. In 1914 he had been commissioned a second lieutenant, a year later first lieutenant. Outside events were shaping Francesconio's future.

On March 15, 1916, on orders from President Wilson, a punitive expedition was formed to retaliate for an attack by some 1,500 Mexicans against Columbus, New Mexico. This incident is of little consequence except that the expedition commander was a fifty-six-year-old brigadier general named John J. Pershing. Pershing was only a captain, though he had been in the army eighteen years. It was Teddy Roosevelt who promoted him, jumping him over the intermediary ranks. This type of promotion prevailed throughout the war because the American Army needed officers. There just wasn't an adequate number. The United States at that time had only 9,000 officers and needed 200,000.

Because of these historic circumstances, Francesconio was promoted to captain; also, he was attached to Pershing's staff. They sailed to Europe on the British ship *Baltic*. Francesconio was unaware that among the hundreds of enlisted men on the boat were two young Marquette honor students whose names were Irwin and Isadore Davidson.

The *Baltic* left New York on May 28 and docked in Liverpool on June 8, an uneventful crossing. The ship encountered no U-boats. In Paris, Pershing's headquarters were set up at the Pépinière Barracks on Boulevard Malesherbes. Francesconio was billeted at the Hotel Continental at 3 rue Castigliore. Later he was transferred to an apartment near the Champs Elysées. (I know because on my honeymoon, a gift from Francesconio, my husband and I looked up the place where Francesconio had been billeted.)

In September 1917, Pershing's headquarters were moved to the field and established at Chaumont, a town on a high hill with rivers on each side. The countryside was mountainous and covered with forests. Chaumont was the historic site of the Treaty of 1814 that sent Napoleon to Elba. From here Francesconio was transferred to a field command with the 26th Division during the Meuse-Argonne offensive. Pont-à-Mousson, which is on the Meuse River and close to Metz, was the scene of fighting between the Germans and the French. It was at Metz that Francesconio's division was assigned to the French Army. The war had created deep hatred, dividing friends, even relatives.

Alsace-Lorraine is a garden of flowers and grapes. Its picturesque towns are often cobbled and gabled, as is Kaysersberg, the town in which Albert Schweitzer was born. If the Germans produced a Hitler, they also produced one of the noblest men of the twentieth century, a man of the highest intellect with a life dedicated to serving the humblest.

One night Francesconio and a unit were assigned to repair a bridge over the river. The plan was to take Metz, and to do so, the bridge was needed. Francesconio sent some volunteer scouts ahead. They reported back that the bridge was unguarded. But the Germans had set a trap, and they were on patrol. They shot and killed a number of the American soldiers. Believing they were all killed, the German patrol went on to the next bridge, a half-mile farther down the river.

The Americans dispersed; they were outnumbered. The instructions were to retreat to safety if they were attacked. Francesconio found himself alone and on a wooded knoll. The night was starless and dark. As he recalled it then, a small hill led back to camp, but in the darkness he could not locate the hill. He hoped the soldiers who had been with him could make it to safety. He heard no sound. If he waited until morning, the Germans would find him and take him prisoner. He debated: would it be better to be taken prisoner, or should he gamble that he could find his way back to camp?

He decided to gamble and began to find his way through the woods and had gone about a couple of hundred yards when he came to the hill. Now, if he could get down the hill, he could find his way, and he would be close to camp. The Germans were not likely to come that close to the French and Americans. But the descent was treacherous in the dark. Francesconio stumbled and fell, rolling down the hill.

When he recovered from the shock, he tried to stand. Then he realized that he was in deep trouble. Something was seriously wrong. He could not stand, and he was in great pain. He tried to roll down the rest of the hill toward a light from a house he could see some distance away.

Perhaps he fainted from the pain. He had no way

of knowing, for when he came to he heard voices speaking in German. He recognized the language, though he could not understand what was being said. Then a voice asked, "Can you stand?" The voice was speaking English. He understood the question but had difficulty in focusing. Where was he and what had happened? He groaned and answered, "I can't stand. Where am I? Who are you?"

His eyes began to focus, and he saw a woman of about fifty looking down at him. "I am a German, and I live in the house which is about a hundred yards from here. Do you think if you leaned on me and my daughter you could hobble to the house?"

Francesconio indicated he would try. Both mother and daughter knelt down and helped him up. The effort to hobble that distance was formidable. Francesconio was in a cold sweat and fell in a faint at the door. The two women managed to get him on a bed and gave him some whiskey and piled some blankets on him after cutting off the top of his shoe. The foot had swollen, and they applied cold compresses to the swelling.

The whiskey made Francesconio drowsy and he fell asleep. A couple of hours later, when he woke, he found the daughter, a girl of about seventeen, sitting next to his bed.

"You are an American captain?"

Francesconio, startled, said, "You speak English. Are you French?"

"No," she answered, "we are German. I learned English at school."

The enemy, thought Francesconio. *I'll be a prisoner —unless they shoot me.*

As though the girl knew what he was thinking, she said, "We will not give you up to the Germans. We are Alsatians and have lived here all our lives. We don't know why we are fighting; the Germans and French have always lived here together. Now neighbors fight against neighbors. My father and my brother are in the army, and the Americans are coming close to Metz. If they win, the war will be over. I don't care if we are defeated."

The girl was bitter. "Why are we fighting? For what and for almost four years? Alsace-Lorraine has been lucky. We haven't lost as many men as Germany has. My brother was taken prisoner, and we don't know where he is. My mother and I will keep you here until the war is over or until American units are close enough for you to get to them.

"We will keep you providing you stay inside so that no one knows you are here. We will wash and dry your clothes inside the house so no one will see your uniform. My mother says your toes are broken and some small bones in your foot. They will heal, but your foot has to be reset when you can get to a hospital."

"What if someone finds me here? Won't you get in trouble?"

"Maybe, but we will take that chance."

Later she told him that many of those living in Alsace-Lorraine were bitter about the war. They could see no reason why they had to fight each other. They didn't care who won, just so the fighting stopped.

They had lived in peace, and now, because of nothing they had done, there was hatred between the Germans and the French. She didn't believe that every Alsatian hated the French, or every Frenchman, the

Germans. Why couldn't they just live as they always had?

In a few days Francesconio was up in a chair and could hobble. The girl found some crutches packed away in the attic; they had been used by one of her brothers years ago. The mother spoke very little English but was quietly attentive to the American captain.

Francesconio assured them that as soon as he could walk, he would leave. At night, when it was dark, he would hobble outside to get some fresh air. The days were tedious and long. What was he doing here? Would he ever get out? Confined as he was to the small house, his usual buoyant spirits were beginning to leave him. He must, he thought, manage to get back to the American lines or he would go crazy.

There was something about the girl which haunted him—her blue eyes, her gold-tinted auburn hair, her slim white neck, her smile. He could swear she resembled Molly enough to be a younger sister.

It was ridiculous, of course, he told himself. It must be because he was remembering and thinking of Molly so often, but it was nevertheless a fact that the girl—whose name was Jennie—resembled Molly. One day she caught him looking at her, and she asked him why he stared at her so often.

"Oh," he responded. "I know a woman in the States whom you resemble so much that it is uncanny."

A few nights later the mother told Francesconio in her limited English that she had two first cousins who had emigrated to the United States. She and their children corresponded often. She wished that her parents had also emigrated, because then she too would have been an American citizen.

Jennie brought out some pictures of their relatives.

"Would the captain care to see them? They had been sent just before the war broke out."

Now Francesconio knew why Jennie looked so much like Molly: the pictures they showed him were of Molly and her sister, Bertha, and her husband, Ben. There she was, Molly, whom he loved, looking lovely even in black and white without her gorgeous coloring.

For the first time in many years Francesconio began to sob. Suddenly his plight—being locked up in that house with two women who were his only protection and who were related to Molly—overcame him.

Mother and daughter were aghast and stood by helplessly. Distraught, Jennie rushed to make some coffee and gave Francesconio a cup. He took her hand and explained why the pictures upset him. So he told them about Molly and the nine boys and how much he wanted Molly to marry him. How he had left without saying good-bye because he was angry, and how he missed Molly.

The fact that he knew Molly put a new dimension into his relationship with the two women. Before he had been a human being who, without their wishes, had become their responsibility. Now it was as though he were a member of the family. Now they told him about the son and the husband who were in the army and how all of them hated it. The father was a skilled mechanic, and the son was a young doctor. Jennie herself had left high school to stay home with her mother. Shortly after, the school was closed. Few teachers were left; they were almost all in the army.

They marveled and so did Francesconio that of all the American officers their cousin's friend should be the one they rescued. The mother shook her head. "It must have been God's will that the American captain should roll down our hill and land practically at our feet."

But Jennie vehemently demanded to know that if it were God's will, why did he allow the war at all? Her mother shook her head—how could she explain God's plans? But Jennie belonged to the generation that demanded answers.

Francesconio was cheered by the news Jennie brought home (she was a volunteer at the hospital). The rumor was that the war would soon be over. It was November 1, and he had been with Jennie and her mother for three weeks. He was eager to leave and get back to the American lines. The Allies were slowly advancing toward Metz, and the German resistance was breaking. He was ready to take a chance to get back to his unit. This time, he believed, because of the rumors that peace was to be declared, he could make it. And he could walk although with a marked limp.

He decided to leave when it was dark, hoping to reach the Allied lines by morning. He said good-bye to Jennie and her mother. He told them that he would never forget them and that he would tell Molly and her family of how they had taken care of him.

When it was dark he began his walk. He made the hill with his foot throbbing, but he was elated that he had encountered no patrols. Now he was sure that with the aid of the cane he carried, he could make it. He had left his uniform behind him with Jennie and her mother. He wore an old suit that belonged to Jennie's father. With his stick and his limp, he hoped that if a German patrol challenged him, his appearance and the few words of German that Jennie had taught him so that he could give his name, and say he was a farmer, would save him.

To return to the Allied headquarters he would have to cross the bridge that his contingent had been trying to take when he broke his foot. The bridge had, apparently, been repaired, either by the Allies or the Germans. He didn't know which. And he had no way of knowing that at that moment the Allies were fighting for the bridge and pushing the Germans back. During the cross fire just eleven feet from the Allied side, a bullet caught Francesconio in his arm and he fell. The Allies gained possession of the bridge; the Germans pulled their wounded back, Francesconio among them. All were taken to the hospital in Metz, and Francesconio once more found himself a patient.

On November 11, the armistice was declared, and the guns that had shaken the world were silenced, though they left the world stained crimson with the blood of the young. Who knows how many potentially great artists, technicians, scientists, died on the battle-field of man's passion for war?

Francesconio developed an infection as a result of the bullet wound, which had been neglected. A fever resulted, and for many days it was touch and go before he was out of danger.

Jennie, who worked in the hospital as a nurse's aide, discovered that Francesconio had been wounded and was in serious condition. She offered to help nurse him, and she knew from the doctors that he was in a grave condition. The infection in the wound was spreading, and they felt there wasn't much hope. Maybe when prisoners were exchanged he would be evacuated from this German hospital. Besides, they sighed, there were so many dying, one more or less—what did it matter? They would do their best, but they didn't know how much hope there was.

Jennie and her mother felt responsible for the American captain not only because they had taken care of him previously but in a way he was a member of their family. When he was better, Jennie's mother said, they must write to their cousin, Molly Davidson.

In Captain Valedara's regiment there was a second lieutenant, Irwin Davidson, who had been separated from his twin, Isadore, who was sent with an American division to England. The young lieutenant knew that Francesconio was in the same regiment, but he had had no contact with him. He also learned that the captain was missing. With some effort he ultimately located the captain, and in the confusion after Armistice Day he found his way to the hospital. He wanted to visit Francesconio.

It was here that he saw Jennie stationed at the admission desk. He was so startled that he stood and stared at her. Jennie too was startled. Why was he staring at her? When Irwin had recovered from his surprise, he explained that she looked so much like his aunt that it was incredible and did she know his aunt, who was the most beautiful woman in the city where he lived?

Irwin explained who he was and that he was looking for Captain Valedara. He explained that because he and the captain had enlisted in Milwaukee, they had been assigned to the same division. He knew that Molly would like to know about the captain. But all the time while Irwin and Jennie were talking he was thinking how pretty she was. She had the same beautiful smile that Aunt Molly had. And what luck to run

133

into her. Now she would take him to see Francesconio.

Francesconio was still delirious and did not recognize Irwin, but Irwin observed that the captain held on to Jennie's hand. Irwin noticed that Jennie bent down to brush Francesconio's hair from his forehead with a tender touch. Irwin wondered whether there was a romance going on between Jennie and Francesconio. After all, Aunt Molly had told him that she had seen Francesconio with other women. So maybe this was another one, proving that he had forgotten about Aunt Molly. Well, when he returned home, he would tell Aunt Molly about his visit to Francesconio. But Aunt Molly had probably forgotten Francesconio by this time. The only thing Jennie forgot to tell Irwin was that she was a cousin of Aunt Molly's.

On such details do the events of our lives hinge. Irwin came to see Francesconio once more but, he had to admit to himself, mostly to see Jennie. This time Francesconio recognized the young lieutenant and Irwin observed that the captain again held on to Jennie's hand.

Well, that was that. She was a beautiful girl, but he was only a second lieutenant and Francesconio was a captain, though from Irwin's standpoint he was pretty old for such a young girl. He must, he reflected, be at least thirty-six or thirty-seven.

C'est la guerre. (That's war.)

18

During these months, Molly was learning more and more about the business of selling dresses. Cynthia taught her a great deal about style, and Molly had a native ability, a flair, and also an outgoing quality of friendliness, for all of which she was promoted to assistant buyer. Management figured that with her extraordinary looks and her personality she could function as both model and buyer.

Mr. Phillips knew that she was persuasive. He never forgot her visit to his office to persuade him to be attentive to Alice. Molly was a rare combination.

When Molly told the boys about her second promotion, they demanded to know what that meant.

"Well," answered Molly, "I still model dresses so that customers can see how they look, but now I tell Mr. Majestic what dresses I think he should order."

"Who is Mr. Majestic?" asked Douglas.

"He's the man who writes down what dresses he thinks he should order."

What they didn't know was that Mr. Majestic didn't want Molly as a buyer. He said he could do the job alone. Besides, he wanted Molly to spend all her time modeling. If Molly modeled a dress, there was no trouble selling it, because Molly looked gorgeous in whatever she was wearing.

"Why," he argued, "should she do anything but model?"

Molly told Cynthia about Mr. Majestic's opposition to the promotion. Cynthia had given the store notice that she was leaving. She had saved enough money to venture to New York, hoping to get a model's job.

"How many dinners," Molly asked her, "did your friends buy for you so that you could save?"

"Every night," said Cynthia, "even including Saturdays. I started three years ago. I have $2,143.62 saved. I deserve a job, Molly, because I had dinner with a lot of creeps. But, mind you, I didn't let them know they were creeps. They got their money's worth. I was entertaining and gay, but that was it—no lovemaking."

Molly looked at her curiously. "So, was there no one you really liked?"

"Sure," Cynthia told her, "but he was poor, and I couldn't afford to go out with a poor man. Nix on that. I want to be a model at one of the big New York stores and earn a lot of money. And let me tell you something, Molly; you are really silly. Why don't you marry Francesconio? He's going to be rich, and you don't want to marry him? That's crazy. If you don't want to marry him, come to New York with me. With your face and some clothes, you'll look like a million dollars, and you can marry a millionaire."

Molly shook her head, "I won't ever get married again."

Cynthia looked at Molly pityingly. "So don't get married. You can get jewels and apartments and all sorts of gifts. Gosh, Molly, don't you know that you are beautiful? I'll tell you what, Molly, when I'm settled in New York and have a job and an apartment, you can come to New York and visit me, and I'll introduce you to some rich men. You tell Mr. Majestic that you want to go on a New York buying trip with him to learn the ropes."

Two months later Molly did go to New York City, which overwhelmed her—its size, its people, its wealth and its style! She practically lost her mind over the magnificent clothes, and Cynthia did give a party and invited Molly, who arrived in a black dress with an enormous velvet hat and a black fox fur.

There was a real whistle when she walked in. By now Molly had learned a few tricks. Not that she needed many—she was a natural coquette. She twisted her lithesome body and smiled radiantly.

"Boy, is she a humdinger," one of the men said to Cynthia. "Has she really been married three times?"

"That's right," replied Cynthia without offering any details.

One of the guests, Jack Rubin, engaged Molly in conversation.

"Mrs. Davidson, you are a beautiful woman, and I'm a busy man."

"So, Mr. Rubin," said Molly, "I'm glad you're busy. That means that you are making a good living."

Mr. Rubin stared at Molly. Making a living! Didn't she know how rich he was? But Molly, ignorant of Mr. Rubin's wealth and vast financial interests, went on blithely: "What do you do for a living? Are you in the suit business?"

"Why should I be in the suit business?"

"Why not? What's the matter with the suit business? You can make a good living providing you don't overstock! Of course if you are not experienced, you won't do so well. Like this dress I am wearing sells for $135. I bought it for $69, so you see the profit in the suit and dress business."

Mr. Rubin was taken aback but in a moment regained his poise. "What did your hat cost?"

Molly leaned toward him and in a low voice said, "You shouldn't ask. I'm wearing it only for tonight. Then it goes back in stock. So does the fur." And Molly smiled triumphantly. "Because," she said, "I didn't want Cynthia to be embarrassed if I weren't stylishly dressed. Besides," continued Molly, "I love them. I love all beautiful clothes. I like to sit at my dressing table and put them on. Before I was married the first time, I worked in a factory, and I hated the factory because it wasn't beautiful and I used to dream of hats like this and furs."

Mr. Rubin was riveted. "Are you married now, Mrs. Davidson?"

"Oh, no," said Molly, "why should I marry again? I've got beautiful things. I don't need to marry, and anyhow, I've been married three times, Mr. Rubin. Three times and no more."

"Why were you divorced?"

"Divorced? Why should I get a divorce?"

"Why did you leave your husbands?"

"What do you mean why did I leave my husbands? I didn't. They left me."

At that moment one of the other guests interrupted, "Come on now, Rubin, you've monopolized Mrs. Davidson long enough. Give us a chance."

Molly moved away from Mr. Rubin and joined a small group.

But Mr. Rubin was fascinated by Molly. She was

honest about her clothes and, apparently, had no idea that he was president of one of the biggest steel mills in the country. She was advising him to go into the suit and dress goods. He was intrigued and stayed until the rest of the guests had left.

"How many invitations did you receive for dinner tomorrow night?" Cynthia asked her.

"I should know," said Molly. "I told them to ask you. How did I do, Cynthia? Was everything all right? Why don't we wash up the dishes now. Give me an apron. Mr. Rubin, you would like maybe to dry for me?"

To say that Mr. Rubin was startled would be to put it mildly. It was many years since he had been in a kitchen much less dried dishes.

"How come, Mr. Rubin, that you don't know you must use a separate towel for the glasses or they won't shine?"

Startled, Mr. Rubin answered, "No, I didn't know that."

"Well," said Molly, tying back her hair with a ribbon as she stood in front of the mirror, obviously, admiring herself, "you should know that a clean and shiny kitchen is a nice thing."

"You are nice and shiny, Mrs. Davidson," said Mr. Rubin.

At this compliment Molly became alert. "Are you married, Mr. Rubin?"

"Why do you want to know?" asked Cynthia.

"Why? Because," said Molly, "you should know, Cynthia, that the whole world is divided into the married and the unmarried. The married I put away to ask how their wife is and how their children are, but for an unmarried man, you should know, Cynthia, it's like a war I like to win."

"Win what?" asked Mr. Rubin, completely befuddled by this Mrs. Davidson.

"Win what?" said Molly, surprised that he didn't know. "It's like a battle. If it's an unmarried man, I want for him to admire me and to say so. That's why God made women soft and pretty. If God didn't intend for women to make men want them, why did he make them weaker and softer than men?"

To this question, Mr. Rubin had no reply. This surely was a woman unlike any he had met before. "But, Mrs. Davidson," he said, "isn't the whole purpose of making women alluring for them to get married?"

Molly yawned, "Mr. Rubin, for you to think that I want to get married is a *mishegoss*. Do you know what that means? It means a craziness. I like to have you think I'm beautiful, and if you want you can send me some perfume—if you've got a job; otherwise, don't—but marriage—not to the best man in the world."

Mr. Rubin was suddenly on the defensive. "What have you got against marriage, and why do you want perfume?"

Molly, now that she was finished washing the dishes, untied the ribbon from her hair, and as it fell over her shoulders, Mr. Rubin had a sudden impulse to bury his head in her hair and kiss her shoulders.

Who knows, thought Cynthia, *whether Molly is doing this deliberately. And yet she is so natural and says whatever she means, so this may not be coquetry but just the way she is. But Mr. Rubin, one of the real catches of the year—divorced, enormously rich and a power in industry, is caught. Imagine him drying dishes! Molly's charm.*

"I want perfume because when a man gives it to me, I know he likes me."

"How many bottles do you own?" Mr. Rubin asked dryly.

Molly began counting on her fingers and then shrugged. "I should know? I use them on the boys' handkerchiefs when they go to Sunday school."

"How many children do you have, Mrs. Davidson?"

With a gleam in her eyes, Molly said, "Nine. May they all live in good health."

Mr. Rubin laughed. "You can't be a day more than twenty-three."

Cynthia spoke up, "She's thirty years old. I know. I was at her house for her birthday."

"Why are you pulling my leg, Mrs. Davidson?"

"Who's pulling your leg, Mr. Rubin? You asked, so I told you. So what do you want of me?"

Mr. Rubin understood that if Molly was telling the truth there must be some explanation. She obviously was too young for nine children, but he was annoyed and made up his mind he would ask no more questions. But as he left he said he hoped to see Molly again.

"Why not?" said Molly with her eyes dancing.

When he left, Cynthia asked Molly why she didn't tell Rubin the truth.

"Well," said Molly, "it's no use telling the truth. Nobody believes me when I tell them I won't ever marry again. Does Mr. Rubin have a job?"

"Molly," said Cynthia, "he's a very, very rich man. He could have bought everyone in this room tonight seven times over."

"So? If he's so rich, why did his wife divorce him?"

"I don't know. He never has said in the few times I've seen him. But he's awful quiet and not much fun."

"If you have so much money," Molly said, "you must worry that no one will take it away, so I don't have such worries. To tell the truth, Cynthia, men can't enjoy money like women because they can't buy beautiful clothes."

The next day when Molly returned to her hotel room after a buying trip, she found a package—a bottle of perfume from Mr. Rubin. Before leaving New York, she obtained his address from Cynthia and wrote him a note of thanks. "You should know," she wrote, "it will be the biggest bottle on my dresser. I'm glad you can afford it. Cynthia says you are rich. Maybe it isn't all so wonderful to be rich, but it isn't all so wonderful to be poor either. Molly Davidson. P.S. The nine boys are stepsons."

Mr. Rubin never forgot Molly, and every so often she would receive a bottle of perfume with a card reading, "For the boys' handkerchiefs." Once he came to Milwaukee and invited her out for dinner. *How beautiful she is*, he thought once again.

"You know, Molly," he said. "I wanted to ask you to marry me, but Cynthia told me you would never marry again."

With a candid smile, Molly answered: "Maybe if you had given me furs and jewels and oceans of perfume, I might have married you, because I love beautiful furs and jewels and the boys would have nothing to worry about."

"So why didn't you tell me you wanted to marry me? You are honest about everything, and surely marriage should be based on honesty."

"Well, you see," answered Molly, "if I had married you, it would have been a sign I didn't love you, otherwise, I wouldn't take a chance that you would die. So, you see, you are really a lucky man."

"I don't see any logic to what you are saying, Molly. If you were running the world, everything would be topsy-turvy."

Mr. Rubin leaned over and kissed Molly. "You are lovely, Molly. If you ever change your mind and decide you love me, let me know."

So Molly stopped at her sister's house after dinner and told Bertha about Mr. Rubin.

My mother was aghast. "*Vay iz mir*. Molly, a rich man—a banker."

"He's not a banker. He makes steel."

"*Nu*, so he's a steelmaker. So, why do you say no to him? You will have to work to support the nine boys all your life. My sister should have such a pack to carry on her shoulders."

Up spoke my father: "Molly, Bertha is right. Where do you find such a piece of gold? He's rich and he's a Jew. How much more do you want? Where will you find such a *mazel* again?"

"I don't like his face."

"So, you don't like his face. You don't have to look at him. Talk to him but don't look."

But my Aunt Molly was perverse this night. "I don't like his voice either. Do me something. I should every day look at him, let him take my hand, come into my bedroom, have him boss the nine boys so I can have furs and jewels? I want I should love him," and thought Molly, *like Francesconio*.

But my mother was shrewd. "It's the Italian for whom you are eating out your heart. A fine man—but he goes away to war and doesn't even say good-bye."

My mother had conveniently forgotten how she opposed Molly's determination to live with Francesconio without marriage.

Molly sighed. Why was everything so wrong in this world? Actually she really liked Mr. Rubin but not for anything serious, for in her heart she knew that no jewels or furs could compensate for Francesconio.

19

It was spring. Francesconio had been released from the hospital and discharged from the army. On the ship that was bringing him back to the United States, he had plenty of time to think. Meeting Jennie and her mother seemed to him to be a message from fate. Now his anxiety was that by the time he returned, Molly would have forgotten him or would be in love with someone else. He had thought of writing to her, but it was too difficult. He had left without saying good-bye, so why should she have given him any thought and what could he say? Ask her to change her mind and marry him?

The first thing he'd better do, he decided, was to rebuild his business. It had been closed during the two years he had been gone, and he was eager to start working again.

He thought often of Jennie and her kindness to him. He told her before he left that he would see to it that she had a trip to the United States. He would never forget the kindness she and her mother showed him. Somehow the whole episode seemed to bring him closer to Molly.

But there remained the nagging feeling that Molly would not change, and what was he to do then? Live with her without marriage?

And Molly had been thinking of Francesconio. She had discovered that if a man and woman lived together as husband and wife and acknowledged it, it would be considered a common-law marriage. In that way, she figured, she would not be offending God by contracting a fourth marriage.

She went to see the Rabbi. He told her that marriage was a sacrament—a total commitment—and that's why a religious ceremony was necessary.

"Maybe," she told him, "that applies to everyone but not to anyone who was married three times and whose husbands died after they married her. But if by living together they were as good as married in the eyes of the state, God would have to understand that she had done what she could."

But when Molly told the Rabbi that she and the Italian were going to be married without a legal marriage, he was appalled.

"Mrs. Davidson," he said, "what kind of an example is this to set for the boys?"

"Rabbi, my boys know all about it. They know how their fathers died early in marriage. They are good boys and they are smart boys, and when they grow up they will get married like I did. They know why I won't marry again."

"But, Mrs. Davidson, if you are not married, what hold will you have on your captain?"

Molly looked startled. "First, you should know, Rabbi, that my Italian is not like that, and second, you should know God wouldn't allow it. It is because of God I'm not marrying him. Didn't God do enough when he allowed my third husband to die? An agreement is an agreement. I told God I would never marry again, because I knew my husband would die. But I didn't tell God I'd never love anyone again. And to tell you the truth, Rabbi, I don't want to live without love."

If she had only known that the Rabbi was thinking: what a woman she was—one surely made for love. And how remarkable to assume the responsibility of nine boys.

"But, Mrs. Davidson, that's a lot of nonsense. God didn't purposely let your three husbands die."

"So was it an accident? God didn't know, who did? Tell me, Rabbi, who did?"

The Rabbi gave up. Mrs. Davidson was too much for him.

In the meantime, Molly was worried about how to handle Francesconio. He had given her up before because she wouldn't marry him. Francesconio had phoned Molly to tell her that he was back and that he had a message for her from a member of the family and would she meet him for dinner?

The day was endless for Molly. There was excitement in the house. The boys knew that she was to meet Francesconio, and Irwin had told her about meeting Jennie, whom Francesconio had seemed so keen about. So Molly thought bitterly that he never could have really loved her. She didn't care about anyone else. She wasn't as fickle as Francesconio, and if he was interested in someone else, why did he want to see her? For that matter, why did she consent to meet him?

Well, why not? Molly said to herself. *What can I lose?*

But Molly's heart was thumping as Francesconio greeted her.

How thin he is! she thought.

My God, she's more beautiful than ever! he thought.

"How are you, Francesconio?" said Molly but thought, *Dear God, why must I want him and no one else?*

"It's been a long, long time, Molly," he said, his mouth dry with excitement.

"So," said Molly, "Irwin tells me you were wounded."

"Yes, my arm is still stiff."

"You were in the hospital a long time?"

"Yes, a long time."

Molly twisted her wine glass. "So you had a good nurse?"

Silence between the two—Molly twisting her glass and Francesconio nervously lighting a cigarette.

"She was maybe a pretty nurse?" inquired Molly.

"Yes, she was a very pretty nurse," answered Francesconio. It had begun to dawn on him that Molly might be jealous, so he played it to the hilt. "Yes, Molly, her name is Jennie and she's very pretty—blue eyes like yours. I don't know what I would have done without her."

"So why did you leave her?"

"Because I wanted to get home to reopen my business."

"So business for you is more important than a woman?"

"It's all right. Molly, she will be coming to the U.S. I hope you will meet her."

"So, Captain Valedara, you ask me to meet you for you are marrying a European girl. You should be happy, and if you'll excuse me, I don't want any dinner. Save your money for dinners when she's here."

Francesconio's face broke into a great smile. Molly was jealous. That was great. He was going to win out. If she loved him enough to be jealous, she surely would consent to a marriage.

"Molly," he said, "Molly, my dear love" and he took her hands in his.

Molly tried to withdraw them. What did he think? He was calling her "his dear love" and bringing another woman to the United States.

"Molly, the woman is a girl about eighteen, and she is your cousin, your mother's sister's daughter, and she looks just like you. Your eyes, your skin, your smile, and she and her mother took care of me."

Molly stared at Francesconio, and tears began to roll down her cheeks. "I thought you were in love with her."

"I'm in love with only one woman, and that's you, Molly."

And then he told her of how Jennie and her mother rescued him and how afterward Jennie nursed him at the hospital and how he had clung to Jennie, who he had thought was Molly when he was delirious with fever, and how he had promised to bring her to the United States for a visit.

"Let's get out of here," said Francesconio as he summoned the waiter. "I want to hold you in my arms."

Once in the car Francesconio took Molly in his arms, who by this time was sobbing. Francesconio held her gently until she quieted. "Molly, will you marry me?"

Molly put her head on Francesconio's shoulder. "I will marry you if it's the only way, but you should know day and night I will worry that you will die, but I will marry you."

That was enough for Francesconio. Molly had gotten over her foolishness, and now this beautiful woman was to be his. If she wanted, they would be married by his priest. Maybe in another ceremony by her Rabbi.

Francesconio was deliriously happy. He drove her home to tell his parents and then to Molly's sister and brother-in-law's. My mother was practically hysterical, having decided that Aunt Molly was crazy. "Now a Catholic!" she moaned to my father. "What kind of life will this be for my sister with the priest and all his Italian friends?" But my father liked Francesconio and pointed out that if Molly could marry a Baptist and an Episcopalian, what was so terrible about a Catholic?

"*Vay iz mir*" ("Woe is me") my mother moaned. "A Catholic is different; they are more gentile than a Baptist."

"Remember," I said, "that doesn't make any difference to Aunt Molly. She thinks all denominations are like political parties and that God doesn't care which one is Jewish or Catholic. They all vote for Him for President."

My father said, "Only my sister-in-law, Molly, would have likened God to the President of the United States."

"It's a *mishegoss*," my mother again moaned.

"Well, at least she's going to have a wedding," I pointed out to my mother, "and that's what you wanted."

20

Plans were made for their unique wedding. "First of all," said Francesconio, "we will have to have a bigger house."

"A bigger house!" Mrs. Kolensky exclaimed. "My knees hurt now. I should have more backaches and more laundry and more floors to mop?" And then piously, "Another *shaygets*."

Douglas confronted her with reproachful eyes, "Well, I'm a *shaygets* too. I'm Episcopalian."

"So you're a *shaygets*. What kind you are makes no difference. I still have to wipe behind your ears to make sure you're clean."

Mrs. Kolensky was assured that someone would be hired to do the laundry.

"But three bathrooms!" she complained, but it was only noise. Mrs. Kolensky was as excited as the boys, and though they would have preferred to have Aunt Molly to themselves, still Francesconio was a nifty guy, and he had one definite asset—his car.

When Francesconio arrived to pick up Molly, his car enjoyed the most careful scrutiny, and when he allowed them to wash the car, he won their hearts completely.

Everybody was happy—Francesconio radiantly so

—except Aunt Molly. She couldn't eat, she slept very little; she became thinner, and her clothes became too large for her. One day while modeling a wedding dress, she fainted.

Francesconio became alarmed. My mother was beside herself. "That's what comes," she pointed out to my father, "of marrying a Catholic. It is making Molly sick."

"Rubbish," I told my mother. "How come Aunt Molly didn't get sick when she married an Episcopalian, and they are first cousins to Catholics?" I said.

My mother just continued moaning. I couldn't tell her—she knew her sister was wasting away because she was going to marry a Catholic.

My father shrugged. "Molly and her sister, Bertha, you should know, my child," he said, "have bricks in their heads. A new idea cannot get through to them."

The doctor came. He examined Aunt Molly and then told Francesconio that Molly was suffering from fear.

"Fear?" Francesconio asked, perplexed.

Fear, the doctor explained, was literally killing Aunt Molly. Fear that if she married Francesconio he would die.

Francesconio was appalled. "It's impossible."

"No, it's not impossible, and I must tell you, Mr. Valedara, that if a woman loved me to such a degree, I'd be damned if I'd insist on a marriage ceremony. You know if you live with her and acknowledge her as your wife and she that you are her husband, the state will look upon you as husband and wife. What God will think about the arrangement I don't know, but if it were me, I'd take a chance with God. If He put the idea in Mrs. Davidson's head, He must have had a reason."

So Francesconio told Molly that he didn't really care if she didn't want a marriage ceremony. It was all right with him. "Suppose," he said, "we just have a dinner for the family and that would be the wedding?"

Molly slept that night for the first time in weeks. Color came back to her cheeks. If she loved Francesconio before, she loved him even more and clung to him, which charmed Francesconio. She wore the big diamond engagement ring, and her smile became more radiant and her eyes sparkled. It was something to see her leave with Francesconio in the car when they went out for the evening.

Molly loved having dinner with Francesconio. She explained to him that having dinner with different men every evening had enabled Cynthia to save almost $3,000, so she was doing the same thing, putting $3 away every night they dined out."

"What are you saving for?"

"Well," answered Molly, "if your business should fail, you would have something to fall back on."

She insisted on continuing her job. She did not want the boys to be dependent on Francesconio.

"Don't worry, Molly, I'm not a poor man and I'm going to make more money, and I'll take care of the boys when their money is used up. I want you all the time, so just give up your job. It will be a big house that I'm building for us, and it will take you time to run it."

So Molly gave up her job—to the distress of the department store. There was no Lib Movement to persuade Molly that her destiny was success in business.

Her destiny, she would have told you, was in Francesconio and the boys. And Francesconio was content. He once told me that his male vanity got a kick out of watching men go goggle-eyed over Molly's beauty. And what's more, he assured me, she never looked at another man.

But I knew my Aunt Molly, and I was sure she enjoyed having men admire her. It had nothing to do with her love for Francesconio, which was deep and unending but didn't stop her from being a coquette. It was part of her lure for Francesconio.

Irwin had come home, walking with a limp and a cane. He would always walk with a limp, but Molly's joy that he had returned from the war made his injury insignificant. "There," she told Francesconio triumphantly, "that was to compensate for his father's early death. God knew what he was doing."

Francesconio, seeing Molly's happiness at Irwin's safe return, announced that he would donate $5,000 to his church in thankfulness for the twins' safe return.

Molly demanded to know why he gave $5,000 to *his* church. "Doesn't Jehovah who brought back the boys deserve some appreciation? You think He will like this?"

"Molly," Francesconio told her, "listen, I'm not like you. I can't go from one church to another as you do."

"So what? I believe in Jehovah. Should I care which church you were baptized in? If you ask me, God doesn't pay any attention to all those different groups. He's too busy with worrying about the whole world."

"So," said Francesconio, "why are you disturbed if I give to my church and not yours?"

Molly might not have been logical by other standards, but she was by hers—so why should you take a chance? "Let God know you support *all* the clubs that belong to His lodge," she said.

Between Molly's ideas of God, the nine boys and his own suddenly booming business affairs, Francesconio gave up. Molly won, and Jehovah's Jewish clubs were $5,000 richer.

21

The boys grew to manhood. Francesconio saw them through college. Robert and Kenneth joined his firm. Irwin went back to Alsace and married Jennie and in due time became a well-known doctor. Isadore passed the bar but never practiced, preferring to teach. Douglas never married but to no one's astonishment became editor of a popular magazine. Donald wrote songs and became an entertainer and appeared in the movies. Molly and Francesconio were invited to Hollywood for the premiere of the movie, and Molly was, as Francesconio noted, more beautiful than the star. Victor and Jonas sold automobiles in partnership and made a fortune.

"God," said Molly, "showed clearly that my adopted sons were particularly protected by Him."

"Which God?" Francesconio teased her. "The Baptist, the Episcopal or the Jewish God?"

Douglas, who was listening, said, "Molly's God doesn't bother Himself about such trifles as the differences between Jews or Baptists or Catholics. In this house, there is a universal church."

"You should know," said Molly, "that Douglas should have been a minister."

"Molly," answered Douglas, "living with you I'm only part Baptist. The rest of me is Jewish and Episcopalian, and with Francesconio here, I've even got a little Catholic in me."

It was something to see all of them together, which happened frequently, for they were devoted to one another. Between the nine boys, their wives, and their children and Bertha and my father and me and, later, my husband, they were noisy, gay and happy get-togethers.

Then Molly was in her element. Francesconio never quite got over his amazement that he had not only Molly but all the nine boys. It was the last kind of life he had envisioned for them, but Molly's magic touched all our lives and made them richer.

On the twenty-fifth anniversary of the day Francesconio and Molly announced that they were going to live together, Molly's boys presented her with a wedding ring studded with rubies.

"Aunt Molly," they told her, "you would never wear a wedding ring from Francesconio, but this ring celebrates the wedding between you and the nine of us. We want you to know that it's been a happy marriage for us, for if it hadn't been for you, we boys would never have met and become like brothers. You gave us a home and your love. Wear this ring with our love."

Molly wept and slipped on the ring next to the diamond engagement ring Francesconio had given her one April night many years before.

The boys maintained their loyalty to one another throughout the years. If one was in trouble, the others all rallied around; if it was a financial crisis or if one of them was ill, they all helped. It was a rare devotion, the result of Molly's influence.

Molly grew more beautiful—her happiness in having Francesconio and the boys in and out of her home made her radiant. Francesconio would sometimes introduce her as "my wife who isn't married to me." His friends knew about her neurosis, and strangers thought it was amusing but not real.

Molly's heart expanded with the years. She shared her happiness with everyone. She babied and fussed over Francesconio—to make up, she said, for refusing to marry him. When his mother was ill, it was Molly who nursed her, and, unbelievably, Francesconio's mother, devout Catholic, offered up prayers to all her saints for Molly.

As Francesconio grew richer, Molly's clothes became more gorgeous, and she along with them.

It was a happy household, and Francesconio remained enchanted with Molly and her unorthodox reaction to life. Strange though it was, as he reflected, it had given happiness to all the nine boys and himself.

For thirty-two years the house grew in warmth and kindness. The boys and their wives and their children were frequent visitors. It was the kind of house that rang with the sound of laughter and conversation and an occasional child's weeping and the sound of dishes and a coffeepot that was always in use. But there came a day when the noise stopped. Molly was ill. Beautiful, loving Molly's heart was beating at a dying pace. Francesconio sat beside her, holding her hand, lifting it to his lips, praying that it would not grow cold.

"Lift me up, Francesconio. Hold me in your arms. Let me look out at the lilac bushes." Francesconio stroked Molly's hair.

Molly is beautiful, he thought. *What happy years. Molly who laughed and loved so much. Holy Christ, don't let anything happen to her.*

soon open wide."

ong pause, Molly stirred. "The blossom

"I will pick some for you, and they can open here on the table. Would you like that, Molly?"

He thought that if he could he would have bought all the lilacs in the world and placed them in her arms to tell her of his love now and forever. She lay with her head on his shoulder. He felt her body so dear to him, so familiar. How many years was it? For thirty-two years she had graced his life with sweetness and with laughter. She denied that she was his wife, but what wife could have been closer than she?

Would he ever forget her shining eyes that night when she became his love and pledged her loyalty to him. His beautiful Molly, his tender Molly, his yielding Molly, his life and his happiness. *Oh, God, save her for me*, he prayed.

Molly slipped her hand into his. "Hold me, Francesconio."

Molly was no longer thinking of the budding lilacs. She was remembering the early years. "You see, my love. God kept his agreement with me. He didn't let you die. How wise I was not to marry you. I will go first. Don't cry, Francesconio. I love you." And in Francesconio's arms, Molly gave her last smile and with a sigh went to meet her God, with Whom she had had a unique personal relationship.

The nine boys stood by Francesconio through the lonely days and years after Molly's death. He was never neglected by the boys, who were devoted to him and Molly's memory. They would go to see him frequently, and often brought their children with them. Often they would reminisce about their first meeting and Aunt Molly's refusal to admit that she loved Fran-

cesconio until the boys had voted their approval. When his will was read, it was the greatest tribute, I think, that any man ever paid a woman.

"My sons," it said, "all nine of them need no money. I have given them an education and they have filled me with pride. But, in the memory of the sweet woman who was my wife in all but legal name, who took those nine boys who were not her own and gave them her heart and allegiance, who would not even accept me unless all nine of them approved of me; in her memory I bequeath my fortune to the homeless orphan children and hope that somewhere they, too, will find love as all of my nine sons did. I know you will not contest this will; and I have, therefore, asked the three eldest to be the executors of my earthly possessions."

That's why I love my Aunt Molly's memory, and that's why I think she was a far greater woman than many who lead what is described as a virtuous life.